Otto Pfleiderer

Philosophy and Development of Religion

Being, The Gifford Lectures Vol. I

Otto Pfleiderer

Philosophy and Development of Religion
Being, The Gifford Lectures Vol. I

ISBN/EAN: 9783337081409

Printed in Europe, USA, Canada, Australia, Japan

Cover: Foto ©ninafisch / pixelio.de

More available books at **www.hansebooks.com**

PHILOSOPHY AND DEVELOPMENT OF RELIGION

BEING

THE GIFFORD LECTURES DELIVERED BEFORE
THE UNIVERSITY OF EDINBURGH, 1894

BY

OTTO PFLEIDERER, D.D.

PROFESSOR OF THEOLOGY, UNIVERSITY OF BERLIN

IN TWO VOLUMES

VOL. I.

NEW YORK: G. P. PUTNAM'S SONS
EDINBURGH: W. BLACKWOOD & SONS
1894

All Rights reserved

PREFACE.

My Gifford Lectures were delivered at Edinburgh in January and February of this year, and I sent them forthwith to press without material alteration or addition. The verbal form alone has been somewhat improved here and there; and some passages omitted from want of time in delivering the Lectures, have been incorporated in the following pages. It seemed to me unnecessary to add anything to what the Lectures originally contained, but I may refer those readers who are further interested in my views to my 'Religionsphilosophie,' third edition ('Philosophy of Religion,' translated from the second German edition, 1886), and to my 'Urchristenthum' (Berlin, 1887).

My hearty thanks are due to Dr Hastie for his translation of the Lectures from my German manuscript, and to Professor Kirkpatrick for his careful revision of the proofs.

OTTO PFLEIDERER.

April 16, 1894.

CONTENTS OF THE FIRST VOLUME.

LECT.		PAGE
I.	INTRODUCTION,	1
II.	RELIGION AND MORALITY,	37
III.	RELIGION AND SCIENCE,	69
IV.	THE BELIEF IN GOD: ITS ORIGIN AND DEVELOPMENT,	102
V.	THE REVELATION OF GOD IN THE NATURAL ORDER OF THE WORLD,	137
VI.	THE REVELATION OF GOD IN THE MORAL AND RELIGIOUS ORDER OF THE WORLD,	170
VII.	THE RELIGIOUS VIEW OF MAN:—	
	I. HIS ESSENTIAL NATURE AND HIS ACTUALITY,	204
VIII.	THE RELIGIOUS VIEW OF MAN:—	
	II. REDEMPTION AND EDUCATION,	236
IX.	THE RELIGIOUS VIEW OF THE WORLD:—	
	I. IDEALISM AND NATURALISM,	267
X.	THE RELIGIOUS VIEW OF THE WORLD:—	
	II. OPTIMISM AND PESSIMISM,	299

PHILOSOPHY OF RELIGION.

LECTURE I.

INTRODUCTION.

I HAVE, first of all, to express my thanks to the Senatus of the University of Edinburgh for the high honour which they have bestowed upon me in choosing me to be the Gifford Lecturer for this year. The greater the confidence thereby reposed in me, so much the more do I feel doubt and anxiety as to whether I shall succeed in completely satisfying this confidence. For it is not an easy matter under any circumstances to speak in a satisfactory way about the highest questions which can engage the human mind, before an assembly like this—composed as it is of highly cultivated hearers of the most varied religious and scientific views; and in the case of a stranger the difficulty is increased in many respects to the highest degree.

Not only must his imperfect mastery of your language compel him to appeal for an indulgent judgment regarding the form of his Lectures, but he also finds himself in a difficult position even with regard to the selection of the subjects to be treated, because he does not possess, like a native of the country, the living feeling that animates his audience, nor does he sufficiently know the interests and questions which are specially prevailing at the time. It is but too possible that he may easily treat in too great detail much that is already known and self-evident to his hearers, and may touch only in a cursory way other themes with regard to which they would specially desire to have more thorough discussion in detail. In these respects I must certainly appeal to your consideration, although perhaps to a certain degree the difficulty is lessened in my case by the fact that, in consequence of several former visits to this city, and of friendly intercourse with some of its social circles, and the amiable hospitality which I received on these occasions, the spiritual life of Edinburgh is not quite strange to me.

I confess that the idea of appearing here, particularly in Edinburgh, as Gifford Lecturer on "Natural Religion," has had for me a peculiar attraction and charm. This city has always had a special interest for me ever since I came to know it, because I saw here the two great living forces of Religion and Science combined with one another, and even rivalling each other, in a degree such as perhaps can be seen nowhere else. And more especially as regards the theme of "Natural Religion," the development of this conception appears to me to be connected in the closest way with the history of the spiritual life of this city. Let me, as witnesses for this view, single out from many others only three names, those of John Knox, David Hume, and Thomas Carlyle.

Perhaps the first of these names will appear to you somewhat paradoxical in this connection. You may ask, What has the Reformer, with his belief in the Bible, to do with "Natural Religion"? Does his glowing zeal for the faith not rather stand as far as possible from the cold scepticism of a David Hume? This question I take leave to answer, in the first place, with this other question, Would such a work as David Hume's 'Dialogues on Natural Religion' have been ever possible in Edinburgh without the work of Reformation carried out by John Knox? If, as I suppose, you will answer this question with me in the negative, you have thereby also already admitted that, notwithstanding all the manifest opposition between these two men, John Knox and David Hume, there does in fact also exist a positive connection between them; nay more, that in the last instance no other than the Reformer of Scotland, with his strong faith, has the merit of the fact that we can to-day in Edinburgh carry on scientific discussions concerning the subject of Natural

Religion. Undoubtedly such discussions would have been to Knox at best a matter of extreme indifference, if not even somewhat of a horror to him. The Reformer, as such, is not a man given to scientific investigation, but to practical action. But as regards Knox's activity, in what else did it consist but in the establishment or restoration of *Natural Christianity?* His object was to free Christianity from the deformations and disguises which it had suffered in the dogmas, worship, and hierarchy of the Roman Church, and to bring its genuine, original, or natural truth in faith and morals again to recognition. Hence he went back from all the conventional traditions and usages of the Church to the historical source of religion, to the Word of God in Holy Scripture, and to the inner testimony of its truth, to the voice of God in the conscience. In the harmony of this inner testimony with that historical testimony the Reformation of the sixteenth century found its fixed point, from which it was able to move the world, to shatter the ecclesiastical system of the Middle Ages, and, by its liberation of the consciences of men from priestly tyranny, also to pave the way for the civil liberty of the peoples.

It was certainly a far way from the natural—that is to say, Biblical—Christianity of the Reformer, to the natural—that is, rational—Christianity of a Locke, Toland, and Tindal, and, finally, to David Hume's 'Dialogues on Natural Religion.' We should never forget that the Reformation of the sixteenth century did not spring directly from an intellectual interest, but from the practical interest to purify the Christianity of the Church from the abuses which had become offensive to the pious conscience. Hence its criticism was directed only against the *ecclesiastical* traditions, and, moreover, against them only in so far as they had become directly prejudicial to the religious and moral life. The Reformation, however, stopped short before the Bible, and indeed even enhanced its infallible divine authority, because it needed this firm support in its struggle against the Roman Church. Besides, it had maintained the old ecclesiastical dogmas regarding the Trinity, the Deity of Christ, the Atonement, Grace, and Election, because it was believed that these dogmas were grounded on Holy Scripture. Thus the faith that proceeded from the Reformation was a mixture of old and new, which indeed indicated a progress in practical respects, yet still contained for the thinking reason as many points of objection as did the medieval scholasticism.

With this halfness the human mind could not permanently stop. When it had once exercised its good right to a critical testing of the traditional on *one* side, what was to hinder it from going still further? The impulses of this movement came from various sides. Natural Science had made powerful progress since the middle of the sixteenth century. The old idea of the world had been overturned by Copernicus; our earth had been removed from its central position, and had been shown to be one of the innumerable revolving bodies in the universe; and thereby the fixed positions of above and below, which constituted the frame of the image of the world according to the old faith, had disappeared. Thereafter the thinking mind penetrated always further into the laws of the universe by its methods of observing, calculating, and experimenting, and with every step in the progress of inquiry it strengthened itself in the conviction not only of the immutable order and regularity of the events that happened in the world, but also of its own capability of ascertaining the truth in all departments by rational thinking. And, in contrast to this proud progress of science, how melancholy was the condition of the life of the Church! Out of the Reformation had arisen various new Churches and Confessions which were engaged in the most violent quarrels with each other and with the old Church; and from the religious confusions of the time there had grown bloody wars, revolutions, and reactions in all countries. The sacrifices required on every side by these religious conflicts were innumerable. In place of the old religious compulsion of the universal Church, there had arisen the not less intolerance of the several religious parties which had attained to political power. Under such impressions the question necessarily and inevitably pressed itself upon thinking men as to whether the distinguishing forms of faith, to which these numberless sacrifices were brought, were of such high value after all. The question was asked whether the truth of Christianity really lies in the mysterious dogmas, about which the believers contended with each other all the more bitterly the less they were rationally conceivable; or whether the truth did not much rather lie in the universal truths about which all are agreed, because reason is able to comprehend their truth.

Founding upon such reflections, Lord Herbert of Cherbury published as early as 1624 his work on 'Truth, and its Relation to Revelation,' in which he presented five "really catholic truths," concerning God, moral worship, and future recompense, and designated them as the true kernel which had been contained in all religions from the beginning, but which had been obscured in the course of time by the fraud or deception of priests. In the same sense John Locke, towards the end of the seventeenth century, wrote his work on 'The Reasonableness of Christianity.' John Toland wrote on 'Christianity not Mysterious'; while Matthew Tindal, in 1730, published his treatise entitled 'Christianity as old as the Creation, or the Gospel a Republication of the Religion of Nature.' The common thought of these writings was, that Christianity is essentially nothing else than the moral religion of reason, the truth of which is to be apprehended by the universal human reason, and which therefore was originally common to all men, but which has been distorted in later ages by manifold superstition. Christianity has, properly speaking, introduced nothing new; it only brought the original true religion of reason again to light by removing the false additions to it; but it soon again fell under the same fate of superstitious distortion by mysterious dogmas.

What gave these men courage for such bold criticism of the faith of the Church was the conviction that what still remained after their criticism—namely, the belief in God and immortality—was irrefragable truth that could be proved by reason with mathematical certainty, and had been possessed by all rational men from the first. It is the merit of David Hume that he subjected this assumption to a dissolving criticism, and thereby carried forward scepticism to absolute doubt. His celebrated 'Dialogues on Natural Religion' (published in 1779, three years after his death) begin with the assertion that the true—that is, the sceptical—philosophy is best at peace with theology, seeing that, next to total ignorance, nothing is so conducive to certainty of faith as the insight that we can know nothing at all, and therefore are reduced to unconditional belief. It is difficult to determine how far he was in earnest with this conclusion; it is certain only that he wished by his frequently-repeated reference to Revelation to secure a justification for the unreserved criticism of the Religion of Reason. It is specially the popular inference from the conformity to design in the world to an intelligent former of the world, against which he advanced a series of acute objections. That inference, he proceeded to say, is inadmissible, because it rests upon the analogy of the origin of the world with the origin of human works of art, whereas the origin of the world is an absolutely singular case or effect, and is not to be judged according to any human analogy. For the world as a whole, the analogy of the natural production and growth of organisms has a nearer relation than that of the artistic making of the objects of human art. Why, then, in attempting the explanation of the world, should we not rather stop at the principle of natural development, than seek a transcendental cause? Hume also referred, at least in passing, to the possibility that the apparent conformity of the world to design might be the consequence of happy accidents, seeing that among the infinitely many possible combinations of the elements of the world one might at last result so happily that the forms which had thus arisen might be able to preserve and constantly maintain themselves. Finally, he asked, With what right can one assume the complete designedness of the world, seeing that men of all ages, and not least the Christian theologians, had yet so much to complain of concerning the universal badness of the world and the endless evils of this miserable life? The actual condition of the world is so far from justifying us to infer a perfect, all-good, and all-wise Author of the world, that, as Hume believes, it might much rather be regarded as the first attempt of a beginner God, or as the weak product of an aged God; nay, even the idea of a plurality of authors, who had mutually impeded each other, appears to him to be a hypothesis worth considering. In any case—this is his result—whether we accept one God, or many Gods, or no God, the world remains always equally inconceivable; and hence any of these views has just as much, or as little, right on its side as the others. The utmost that we can assert is the probability that the cause, or the causes, of the order of the universe may have a remote similarity with human intelligence,—a proposition which, as Hume very rightly remarks, is much too indefinite to suffice as the principle of a practical religion.

A similarly negative result is also reached by the criticism of the proof of Immortality, as Hume has treated it in his essays on Suicide and Immortality. The popular proof from retribution rests on an inadmissible introduction of juridical points of view into morals, and on the unjustified assumption that retributive justice, because it does not sufficiently exhibit itself in this world, which is known to us, must work so much the more certainly in a future world. Our present experience shows us a certain retribution in the natural inward and outward consequences with which virtue and vice are wont to be accompanied. But above all this there is still a something further to be desired, or rather required—namely, that the constitution of the world should direct itself according to the wishes of our supposed standard reason. But that there lies a guarantee for immortality in the instinctive desire of the human soul for infinite development, is not admitted by Hume, since our capacities hardly appear to be sufficient for a tolerable life in time, and much less for a whole eternity. On the contrary, he finds in the powerful instinct of the fear of death an urgent warning of Nature against illusions with regard to the life beyond. In no case, therefore, can the belief in immortality be supported upon rational grounds, but only upon the revelation of the Gospel.

If, then, the grounding of religion upon reason is in every respect as problematical as Hume's criticism sought to prove, the question arises, How is it to be explained that religion could take rise at all, and become such a powerful force in human history? Hume has sought to solve this question in his work on 'The Natural History of Religion.' It is not the powerless reflections of reason which are the roots of religion; but, says Hume, the energetic and irrational passions of the soul, and fictions of the imagination or fantasy, fear and hope, drove men from the beginning to seek their Gods behind the unknown forces of Nature on which their weal and woe depend; and in this process the fantasy, in virtue of its anthropomorphising tendency, personified the manifestations of Nature. Hence it follows that the oldest form of religion was not Monotheism, and therefore that the primitive religion was not (as the Deists supposed) identical with the Religion of Reason. As little as men cultivated geometry before agriculture, just as little had they, before the development of civilisation in the primitive prehistoric times, already a Monotheistic knowledge of God. The primitive men much rather thought of their Gods as powerful beings like men, but neither almighty nor morally good. When, then, one God was gradually raised above the others, and especially when the God of a particular people was elevated above those of other peoples, and when, in order to win his favour, more and more flattering expressions of honour were attributed to him, at last there was reached the idea of an infinite God. Religious Monotheism is therefore, according to Hume, just as little as religion in general, a product of reason, although it coincided accidentally with the thought of God maintained by the philosophers. Besides, the more sublimely Monotheism is conceived, it does so much the less permanently satisfy the need of the multitude, who would fain represent the divine in more vivid form and in more intimate relation; and hence they have recourse to intermediate beings, which, as representatives of the highest God, now take up his place, and thereby the old Polytheism returns anew.

Thus, according to Hume, the history of religion moves in a constant wavering or oscillation between Monotheism and Polytheism, the advantages and defects of which maintain a certain reciprocal equilibrium between them; and, indeed, the barbarism of Monotheistic intolerance and its tendency to persecution is, says Hume, even worse than the crudeness of the heathen forms of worship. Generally it appears to him that the influence of the popular religion upon morality is exceedingly unfavourable. The crude notions of the divine arbitrariness and of the torments of hell have a hardening effect upon the soul; and worst of all is the delusion that the favour of the Deity is not to be deserved by right conduct but by ceremonial observances, whereby morality is desecrated and the morals of a people are undermined. Thus religion, like all other things, has also its two sides; and it is difficult to say which of the two predominates in the common actuality of life.

While we are far from being able to concur in this radical scepticism, which saw in religion only an irrational pathological phenomenon, yet this must not hinder us from recognising the significance of Hume for the science of religion. By his logical criticism he has destroyed the self-sufficient dogmatism of the period of rationalistic enlightenment, whose half-criticism was neither just to faith nor to knowledge, because it imagined that it exhausted all reason in its narrow intellectual conceptions, and had no sense or comprehension either for the unconscious reason of the religious feelings and symbols, or for the development of reason in the history of religion. It has no longer been possible since Hume to speak of "Natural Religion" in such a sense as if there had been in the beginning of the human race a religion common to all, and consisting of a few simple truths of reason. To have destroyed for ever this illusion of the older rationalism is Hume's abiding merit. He has thereby paved the way for a mode of consideration which seeks and finds the natural, not outside of but *in* the historical, and the rational not outside of but *in* the actual. One of the most thoughtful representatives of this point of view was the historian Thomas Carlyle, who was also so closely connected with Edinburgh. But the way from Hume to Carlyle leads through the German idealistic philosophy.

Immanuel Kant was, according to his own confession, awakened out of his dogmatic slumber by David Hume. In his criticism of the old metaphysical proofs of the existence of God, he followed pretty closely the footsteps of the great Scottish sceptic. But whereas Hume stuck fast in the negation of dogmatism without being able to find a new position, Kant found such a position in the Practical Reason. The Unconditioned, which, according to Kant also, is unknowable by our theoretic thinking, he found given in our moral self-consciousness, not as absolute being, but as absolute obligation, or as a demand of reason to recognise the end of humanity in every man as of absolute worth. This obligation raises our existence above the conditioned phenomena of the world of sense, and makes us citizens of the intelligible world of freedom, or of the spirit. From this fact of our inner moral experience Kant has also derived the content of our religious consciousness—the "moral faith of reason," as he called it—in distinction from all authoritative reason that rests on merely external and statutory grounds. Morality becomes religion, says Kant, when what it teaches to be recognised as the final end of man is, at the same time, thought as the final end of the supreme Law-giver and Creator of the world, or God. This religious view of our duty is indeed not needed for the grounding of our consciousness of duty, which rests exclusively upon the self-legislation of our reason ; but it is certainly required as a guarantee for the possibility of our fulfilment of duty. The presuppositions without which the fulfilment of our moral destination would not be thinkable are demands or "postulates" of the practical reason. Because the moral law is not realisable in any given time without remainder, its realisation, according to Kant, thus postulates an infinite duration of the personality, and therefore immortality. And because the highest good demanded by reason also embraces, along with perfect virtue, a corresponding happiness, which we ourselves are not able to bring about, we have thus to accept the existence of God as a guarantee for the possibility of the attainment of the highest good. Literally understood, this deduction appears to come to this—that we believe in God in order to be able to hope for a future reward of our virtue by happiness; and thereby the belief in God would be grounded upon the eudæmonistic passions of the soul. The rational justification of this position is subject to all those doubts which Hume's criticism had so acutely brought into prominence. But this was not properly Kant's opinion; he wished to show that the belief in God is a necessary demand of our *reason*, of our *moral* self-consciousness, not of our sensibility. Underlying his deduction there was concealed the deeper thought (which appears more distinctly in his 'Critique of the Judgment') that we feel ourselves bound as moral beings to a moral world-order, which is grounded not merely in us but in God, and that the whole course of the world in nature and history is the means arranged by God for the fulfilment of our moral final end. This thought formed thereafter the standing theme of the idealistic philosophy which followed that of Kant.

By this moral issue Kant also made the specific Christian doctrines of sin and redemption more intelligible than the earlier rationalism had done. Although he did not yet reach the full sense of these doctrines, he interpreted them as moral allegories relating to the states of the moral individual. He expounded this view in his work entitled 'Religion within the Limits of mere Reason,' where he says that at the beginning there rules in every one a radical propensity of self-love as the consequence of an inexplicable intelligible act of freedom. The overcoming of this evil principle can only take place through a complete revolution of the disposition, or a "regeneration," which is likewise the business of the individual freedom which *can* triumph over the evil because it *ought*. The historical Jesus comes into consideration in this regard only as an illustrating example of the moral ideal. The proper object of faith, however, is not anything historical, but the moral idea of man which is grounded in our reason. Whoever recognises this ideal, and makes it his supreme principle, is just before God in spite of defects in his individual acts. His earlier trespasses are also made up for, not indeed by a vicarious suffering on the part of another, but really by this, that the new man in ourselves continually suffers, as it were, vicariously for the old man, who alone had deserved the suffering.

It was certainly an important step in advance when Kant strove to find a rational moral meaning, not only in the faith in God, but also in the ecclesiastical doctrine of redemption. But what still prevented him from penetrating into the full sense of this cardinal Christian doctrine was the individualism which he shared with his whole century. He could think of the victory of the good over the evil principle only as a process within the individual subject, and as a work of the subjective reason of the individual; and he was even compelled to confess that this process is inexplicable as an act of the freedom of the individual. But, at the same time, as Kant himself had designated the good as the end of God in the world, it was a small step to seeing that the victory of the good over the evil is not the work of the subjective reason of the individual, but is the advancing work of the universal reason, or of the divine spirit in the historical humanity. When the post-Kantian philosophy took this step, it broke through the limits of the earlier subjective rationalism; it awakened the sense for the objective reason in the great historical life of humanity; and it thereby also overcame the opposition between rational religion and historical religion.

This important turn in the course of our philosophical thinking took place just about the end of the eighteenth and the beginning of the nineteenth century, in the philosophy of Fichte. After this disciple of Kant had carried out his objective idealism with more logical sequence, and had driven it to the utmost point, he recognised the impossibility of stopping at the human Ego as ultimate, and went back to the infinite reason, whose eternal divine life obtains manifold manifestations in the whole realm of finite spirits. With this turning round from subjective to objective, or absolute, idealism, the place of the moral religion of reason was now taken up by religious mysticism, which no longer postulates a distant God for the sporadic supporting of our need of help, but feels the active presence of the divine spirit in the heart of the individual himself. In the work entitled 'Guidance to the Blessed Life,' Fichte described religion as the view of the world which rises above morality, which perceives the divine life in all the manifestations of the true and good, and feels it in one's own self as the power of holy living and loving— as a calm inner mood in which man feels himself animated by God's spirit, and surrenders his selfhood to God's will, and from which there springs joyous and active love of one's neighbour.

This religion of the heart, which Herder had already opposed to the religion of reason, was made by Schleiermacher the theme of his celebrated 'Discourses on Religion to the Cultivated among its Despisers.' Religion, he showed, is neither knowing nor doing, neither metaphysics nor morals, neither dogma nor worship, but it is our pious feeling in so far as we become conscious in it of the connection of our life with that of the All; or, as it is expressed in Schleiermacher's System of Doctrine, it is our "feeling of absolute dependence," in which we take ourselves along with all else that is finite, and refer ourselves to the one infinite cause of the universe. The doctrines connected with religion are secondary products of reflection about the feelings, and means of expression for the communication of them to others; but they do not belong in themselves to the essence of religion. According to Schleiermacher's opinion, one may have much religion without needing the conceptions "miracle, inspiration, and revelation"; but whoever reflects upon his religion inevitably finds these conceptions upon his way. Hence they have an unlimited right in religion, but also only as religious expressions for subjective states of the soul, without their significance being entitled to be extended to the sphere of knowing, or moral acting. Schleiermacher likewise believed that as regards the conceptions "God" and "Immortality," the very same holds good as of all religious conceptions and doctrines: that their theoretical apprehension is not of such essential significance for religion as is usually supposed. The main thing, according to him, is that one should live at all times in the eternal and have God in his feeling, whatever view may be entertained regarding the immortality of the future, and regarding the personality or impersonality of God. Actions do no more immediately belong to religion than do conceptions and doctrines; religion much rather invites one to a quiet passive enjoyment than incites to outward activity. Feelings and actions form two series, proceeding side by side with each other; nothing is to be done *from* religion, but everything *with* religion; the religious feelings ought to accompany the active life uninterruptedly, like a holy music.

Notwithstanding the one-sidedness of this theory, which would make faith the one and all in religion, and in which the influences of the then dominating romanticism betray themselves, yet its epoch-making significance for the science of religion and theology is not to be underestimated. Schleiermacher, by making religion in general, and Christianity in particular, to be understood as a mode of feeling or as a fact of the inner experience, removed the grounds of the conflict between the supra-naturalists and the rationalists regarding the derivation of the dogmatic propositions —namely, as to whether they are derived from reason or from revelation. He set himself in opposition to the supra-naturalists, by apprehending the Christian faith not as a doctrine founded upon external authority, but as an inner determination of our own self-consciousness, which must stand in connection and harmony with the other contents of our rational consciousness; and therewith Schleiermacher also introduced into theology the fundamental thought of idealism, that the mind is able to recognise as truth only that in which it finds its own nature again. On the other hand, he opposed to the rationalists the view that the Christian faith is not a product of rational reflection, but is a modification of the soul, a feeling which is given before thinking and independent of it, and indeed as a fact not merely of individual experience, but of the common experience of the historical community which is called the Christian Church. All Christian doctrines will only be descriptions of the common feeling of Christendom, which is determined by the opposition of sin and redemption, or of the restraint and liberation of the God-consciousness. Redemption is therefore, according to Schleiermacher, as well as according to Kant, not a single miraculous process that occurred once for all in the past, but it is the inner experience of the victory of the spirit over the flesh—of the advancing, strengthening divine principle in man—which is repeated again and again in the pious. But this experience has its active ground, not in the freedom of the individual, as Kant would have it, but in the common spirit of the Christian community, which has proceeded from the historical personality of Jesus, the founder of the community. Thus did Schleiermacher connect again the bonds between the subject and historical Christianity, which had been torn asunder by Kant. Instead of shutting up religion "within the limits of mere (subjective) reason," he put it into the universal connection of the whole life of humanity, and sought to comprehend it as the product of the objective reason in history.

Schleiermacher, however, did not yet carry out logically the fruitful thought of the "development" of religion, seeing that he removed the founder of Christianity to a position above the plane on which the historical humanity moves, and he carried him back to a miraculous origin, thereby opening to supranaturalism the entrance anew into the system of doctrine. This defect was amended and corrected by the Hegelian philosophy of religion. The strength and merit of the Hegelian philosophy lay in this, that it applied the idealism of the Kantian subjective philosophy to the historical life of humanity, and has understood that life in the light of a development of the spirit in conformity with law. Thereby this philosophy made an immense impression upon its contemporaries, who believed they found in it the word that solved all riddles. In this celebrated proposition of Hegel, "The rational is actual, and the actual is rational," there was expressed an optimistic belief in the rational sense and the purposeful meaning of the history of the world—a belief which was a perfect consolation to a generation that was weary of conflict, and which was, at the same time, a wholesome medicine for its idealistic extravagance. Hegel recalled his contemporaries from the Utopias of the golden ages in the past and future, in which the Rousseaus, Herders, and Kants had revelled, to the solid ground of the historical life; and he showed them that undreamed-of treasures of rational ideas and of impelling and active ideals here presented themselves to the eye that was lovingly turned in that direction. He showed them how the reason that governs the world had been able to carry through its sublime purposes in every age and in the case of every people, although half unknown to men themselves; and how even the defects and evils of every time had been only the necessary means of carrying forward the stage that had been reached to a still higher and richer development of the spiritual life of the peoples and of humanity. Thereby a knowledge of history was gained which far excelled all that had been hitherto reached in impartiality and justice of judgment, and in comprehension of the connection of the individual and the whole —in short, in rational objectivity; and this view superseded the rationalistic pragmatism of the eighteenth century, by substituting for it a truly historical method.

This thoughtful view of history was fraught with special advantage to the history of religion and to the Church. Hegel recognised in this history a regular development of the divine revelation in the human consciousness of God, a development in which no point is entirely without truth, yet in which no one point is the whole truth, but in which the divine truth gradually unveils itself more purely, more spiritually, and more clearly to the human consciousness. The historical religions are accordingly neither inventions of human arbitrariness nor the expression of the accidental feelings of pious souls, but are the necessary products of the specific common spirit of the peoples, in the same way as are law and morals, art and science; and they are, therefore, likewise only to be understood in closest connection with the universal history of civilisation and culture. Christianity, however, according to Hegel, is "the absolute religion," because in it the truth of God as the Spirit has become manifest and revealed; man has become conscious of the presence of God in his spirit, and has thereby come to his true freedom in God. Moreover, the process of the evolution of the religious spirit goes further within Christianity; because its true essence can only be realised gradually and in constant conflict with half-truth and one-sided apprehension of truth. To show this teleological rationality in the history of religion, and to overcome thereby the proud subjectivism of the period of enlightenment which had set itself above the historical by its utter lack of understanding and piety—this was the intention and the merit of the Hegelian philosophy of religion. But its defect was its one-sided intellectualism,—its mistaking the fact that religion is not, like philosophy, a thing of the thinking but of the emotional spirit, and that even thoughts only obtain religious significance by their exciting feeling and will, by their determining the disposition of the whole man, and by giving themselves abiding expression in his moral character. So far, Hegel's religion of reason needed correction by the religion of the heart as expounded by Fichte and Schleiermacher.

It is just this combination of Hegel's historical evolutionism with Fichte's ethical idealism that is represented in a classical way by your gifted countryman Thomas

Carlyle. He was one of the freest spirits of our time; his keen critical understanding bowed down before no external authority, no traditional system of belief. In the dogmas and rites of all the Churches he recognised the natural products of the historical stage of culture reached by the peoples; to him they were the symbols in which the eternal idea must clothe itself for the consciousness of every age. But as is the case with all that is historical, much must also again become antiquated when the growth of time has gone beyond them. In his fundamental aversion to all religious formalism, to overestimation of what is statutory and conventional, and to all ecclesiastical form and sham, he may appear at first sight as a radical sceptic, as a second David Hume. And yet no one was further from the empty scepticism of the cold understanding than Thomas Carlyle, whose soul glowed with enthusiasm for the true and good, who bowed in reverence before the great personalities of history, in whom he recognised prophets of the true and heroes of the good. To deny and combat what is false, to believe and to honour what is true, as that in which the eternal God reveals Himself to us,—this was Carlyle's element of life; it was his religion. Has not this pathos of moral idealism the closest affinity with religious enthusiasm, with the courage that sustains the conflicts and sacrifices of the Reformers? In fact, Thomas Carlyle's character appears to stand much nearer that of John Knox than that of David Hume; or rather it may be said that Thomas Carlyle united in himself the religious reverence of the Reformer with the intellectual clearness of the modern thinker who does not fear even the sharp edge of criticism, because he knows that it is the indispensable means of penetrating from what merely seems true to what is genuinely true.

In the spirit of Carlyle, which combines the courage of the thinker in the cause of truth with the reverence of faith, Lord Gifford, the estimable founder of the Lectureship which has brought us together here, wished to see the question of religion treated. And I do not know how they could be otherwise treated successfully. The more we are filled with a sense of the incomparable worth of religion, and especially of our Christian faith, so much the more must we feel it to be incumbent upon us to overcome the impediments which have sprung up in the way of the faith from the scientific view of the world of the present day. For this end it is necessary to show that the doubts of the thinking mind do not affect the *essence* of the Christian faith, but apply only to the *forms* in which earlier generations have set forth this faith,— forms which sprang from and corresponded to the state of culture and the philosophy of former ages, but which on that very account cannot be any longer sufficient and authoritative for the advanced knowledge of our time. It will be a part of the task of these Lectures to show how these forms of faith have taken shape and developed themselves in the course of the ages, what they signify, and what religious truths they would symbolically express. First of all, however, we shall have to make intelligible what the essence of Religion is, which lies at the basis of these changing forms of the doctrines of religion. But in thus proceeding we shall not fall back again into the error of the old rationalism—namely, of seeking the essence of religion in its initial state, or in a so-called "Natural Religion," which was held to consist in certain presumably rational universal truths, but which in truth are only abstract and colourless conceptions. David Hume, as has already been observed, irrefutably showed that there has never been such a natural religion of reason; but irrational passions of the heart and fictions of the imagination were recognised by him as forming the beginning of religion, and the historical investigations since his time have always only more confirmed this view. But from the fact that the condition of religion at the beginning of its history was everywhere more or less irrational and pathological, is the inference at all to be justified that the essence of religion also consists in irrational wishes and dreams? Such a conclusion could only be held to be correct by one who had taken no notice of the great thought which gives the whole science of nature and history in the nineteenth century its proper and specifically distinguishing characteristic in contrast to the enlightenment of the eighteenth century—namely, the thought of *development*.

We know that every living thing unfolds its essential nature only in the whole course of its life, and hence that its state at the beginning least enables us to obtain a knowledge of its real nature. Whoever would describe the essence of the oak, will not derive its marks from the acorn, but from the full-grown tree; and whoever would obtain a knowledge of the essence of man, will not limit himself to the observation of the infant, nor will he choose as his models the savages who are to be found in the crude state of nature. On the contrary, he will give heed to what the human race has developed itself into in the course of thousands of years; and in the highest representatives of the moral and intellectual culture of man he will find the criterion by which to judge of what the human species is by its constitution, or what its essence contains in itself. In like manner, the political philosopher who would determine the essence of the State will no doubt cherish a historical interest in the first beginnings of the historical organisation of humanity, but he will guard himself against defining the conception of the State, as we know it to-day, according to its first crude beginnings; nor will he derive the facts of moral right and the function of the State from the mode of its historical origin, but rather from the conditions and demands of our rational spirit, which has attained to clearness regarding itself by historical experience. The same holds good of Religion: its essence is least of all to be recognised in its historical beginnings; it reveals itself only through its actualisation in the course of its historical development, and most distinctly on the highest culminating point of that development, in Christianity. Only in so far as we give heed to the sum of the religious experiences of humanity as they culminate in Christianity, shall we be in a position for understanding objectively the essence of religion; and if we were to turn away from history, the great teacher in this sphere, we should not get beyond arbitrary hypotheses and empty abstractions.

Assuredly we ought not to forget that even Christianity as a historical phenomenon is not a simple quantity, but a very complicated whole, composed of the most manifold elements. Thus the question immediately arises, Which of these manifold elements are essentially religious, and which of them belong not to the essence of religion but to its more outward vestment, and even to its deformations? Or in other words, In what features of Christianity is religion presented to us in its purest and most valuable development, and in which as less pure and less valuable?

Now it is clear that the relative value of individual historical appearances is only capable of being judged by reference to a universal principle, which contains the ground and law of all that is particular. If, then, religion is a universally human phenomenon, its principle can only lie in the universal essence of man, in what distinguishes him from the lower animals, and therefore in his rational endowment. The principle of religion cannot consist in individual rational judgments, propositions, or doctrines, as was maintained by the old rationalism, but must consist assuredly in reason itself. It will be the task of the next following Lectures to show that reason is so constituted in us that the consciousness of God necessarily proceeds out of its normal function, and to explain what position this consciousness occupies in the whole of our spiritual life in relation to its other functions. To-day it will only be possible to indicate in an introductory outline of our views the leading fundamental thoughts, the further exposition and establishment of which will have to occupy us in the later lectures of this course.

Reason is the synthetic thinking which arranges the manifold contents of consciousness by reference to the unity of the Ego. As theoretical reason, it arranges the mental representations; as practical reason, the appetencies and desires. The harmonious ordering of the representations is the Idea of the true; that of the desires is the Idea of the good. Now, since reason as theoretical and as practical is one and the same reason, it must strive after a supreme unity which comprehends under itself the Ideas of the true and good; and this is the Idea of God. It is only through reference to the Idea of God that the Ideas of the true and good receive their full objective significance. For, as our representations of things in themselves or of the world, their ordering in our consciousness can only be effectuated under the supposition that the world of things is likewise subject to a similar order, or is arranged by a reason similar to ours. The truth of our rational thinking thus assumes the truth of the rational order of the world—that is, of God. And seeing that the desires of each individual are conditioned by those of other men, and also by the nature of things, the harmonious order of the desires in the individual consciousness is only to be attained under the assumption that the same ordering principle also rules in other men and in nature; and thus the realisability of the Idea of the good presupposes the reality of the moral order of the world, or of God. The Idea of God, therefore, contains not merely the finishing unity or highest synthesis of the contents of consciousness within the subject, but also its unity with the trans-subjective or objective world of the real; it guarantees the objective truth of our rational thinking, and the objective realisability of our rational willing.

To the two sides of the Idea of God, in so far as it is the principle of the true and the good, or the highest law of being and of the being that ought to be, there also correspond the two sides which we have to distinguish in religion as the practical relation of man to the Idea of God. The fundamental feeling of religion is best expressed in the words of Goethe,—

"Small do I feel myself within the infinitely great."

This is the feeling of finiteness and limitedness, of *dependence* on an infinitely superior power, against which we can do nothing, and by which our existence and our weal and woe are conditioned. But the religious feeling is not a mere feeling of dependence; it is not a slavish fear of an extraneous mysterious power: where it thus appears we judge it to be a deformity or malformation, a crudeness or degeneration of the religious feeling. Already by the very fact that we know our dependence, or our limit, we are in a certain sense above it; when we make the infinite power on which we feel ourselves dependent the object of our thinking, it appears no longer as entirely strange, but as related to ourselves, as a spiritual power, as the ordering principle of all that is capable of being known by us of the laws, purpose, and beauty of the world, and as what excites our wonder and reverence. Reverence is the feeling of dependence on one who is such that we feel ourselves at the same time sympathetically drawn to him ; and thus it leads over to the other side of religion. In so far as we see in God the good, or the ideal of our true willing, He is the goal of the longing of our *freedom*, which can only be released from the pressure of the finite in that it raises itself from all limited and divided willing to the *one* perfect and harmonious willing of the whole, in order to realise and satisfy itself in surrender to it. From the beginning, mankind have seen in the divine not merely the power on which they feel themselves dependent, but at the same time the ideal goal of their longing, the ideal of their imperfect being, the perfect fulfilment of their highest hopes, the source of their blessedness. Thus, in the religious feeling there comes to be added to the depressing feeling of dependence, elevating *trust* and free self-surrendering *love*. The feeling of dependence, however, is not thereby in any way abolished, but, on the contrary, it only then truly becomes morally deepened. For, when man comes to know God as the good, as the ideal of true willing, he feels himself not merely dependent in his being on divine power, but also bound in his willing to the divine will, and under obligation to obey and serve it; he recognises in the purpose of God, or in the universal good, the regulating rule of authority for his conduct and his judgment of himself. And when he now recognises the distance of his being from this sublime obligation, the humble feeling of human weakness becomes a painful feeling of guilt and unworthiness. But out of this deepest humiliation there springs up again the highest elevation — namely, the desire for liberation, not merely from the pressure of the finite world and its evils, but still more from the dividedness of one's own being, from the pain of the feeling of guilt, and from the weakness of the will to do good. This moral yearning for freedom reaches its fulfilment in the full moral surrender of the individual's own will to the divine will of goodness. In obedience to God man finds his true freedom; out of the humility which overcomes itself there grows the courage of the trust which overcomes the world. The more, in any religion, these two sides of humility and trust, surrender and elevation, dependence and freedom, come to full and harmonious realisation, so much the more does it correspond to the essence of religion, and so much the more does it realise fellowship with its infinite ideal implanted in the essence of the human spirit. In this we have the criterion by which we are able to estimate the relative value of the historical religions, and by which we can understand the law of their teleological development. Hence we shall no longer seek "natural religion" in the rude beginnings of history, and just as little in meagre abstractions from actual religion, which have never been actual; but we shall find them where religion has historically unveiled its true nature, as it alone corresponds to the essence of man—namely, in Christianity.

LECTURE II.

RELIGION AND MORALITY.

THE assertion now often heard that Religion and Morality stood originally in no connection with each other, is an error which arises from a false way of putting the question. Our present moral convictions are taken as a standard, and it is asked whether the oldest representations of the gods correspond to *our* moral ideals, and whether the duties required at the first by religion correspond to *our* conception of duty? As, of course, there is no such correspondence in these cases, it is believed that any original connection between morality and religion must be denied. In maintaining this view, it is forgotten that the primitive morality is just as different from our morality as the primitive religion is from our religion. But it is an incontestable fact that the primitive morality stands in very close connection with the primitive religion, and indeed that the beginnings of all social customs and legal ordinances are directly derived from religious notions and ceremonial practices.

The family is the oldest religious community, and only as such did it become a moral fellowship. The worship of the house-gods or of ancestral spirits was the ideal bond which connected the members of the household into a lasting fellowship regulated by fixed rules. By the entrance of the wife into community of worship with the husband, marriage became sanctioned—that is, it was elevated from a mere natural relationship to a moral relationship, with lasting duties and rights. The paternal authority had its ground, as well as its limit, in the religious position of the father of the family as the performer of the rites of domestic worship. The inalienability of the family property also rested on a religious sanction; for it was not the present living members of the family who were regarded as the legal possessors of this property, but it belonged to the house-god, who represented the enduring unity of the family. The generations of the family had only the usufruct of the property. Again, because the religion of the primitive period was limited to the worship of the house-gods, the circle of moral obligation was likewise still limited to the family; but within these narrow limits the religious faith operated as the motive of moral feelings. As the members of the family felt themselves bound together by the powerful bond of their belonging to the same house-deity, they learned mutually to esteem and love each other. Their natural inclinations and mutual need of help thus received the higher consecration of *piety* through the religious idea. Thus the foundation of morality was laid primarily in the narrowest circle by the religious sanction. The expansion of this narrowest social combination into the form of civil society followed hand in hand with the expansion of the religious ideas and usages. As the members of the family assembled around the household hearth and invited the house-gods, by oblations and invocation, to the common meal, so the community of the city was the union of those who honoured the same protecting deities of the city at the same altars and through the common sacrificial meal. What from the beginning formed the bond of civil society was not interest, nor an arbitrary contract, nor an accidental custom; but it was the sacred repast in presence of the gods of the city, that symbol of an inner union of all the individual citizens bound by their common obligation to an ideal principle, a super-sensible obligatory power. Like the house government of the paternal power, the civil government was originally an efflux of religion, and not a product of force nor of free compact. The royal power and authority were also originally derived from the worship of the public altars, and hence the kings were called Ἱεροὶ, Διογενεῖς. The oldest laws and legislative assemblies were referred by all the peoples back to divine revelation—a correct reminiscence of the fact that they had not arisen from arbitrary invention or agreement, but were regarded as the expression of religious convictions, whose involuntary presuppositions were regulative for the formation of the several relations of life. The laws, like the faith and worship, were likewise a sacred tradition indissolubly connected with the holy places and legends of the community of the city. Religion was mixed up with all the actions of peace and war. It regulated all the manners of the house and of the city, the meals and festivals, the assemblies of the people and the tribunals of justice, the military expeditions and the conclusions of peace,—all these stood in the closest relation with the religious presuppositions and purposes. The moral was not yet distinguished from the religious.

As religious motives lay at the basis of morals and morality from the beginning of civilisation, these again reacted so as to ennoble religion. It is not to be supposed that religion, in order to work as a morally educative power, must have contained from the beginning ideal notions of the nature of the Deity. This was impossible: for whence could men have obtained a knowledge of moral Ideals before they had themselves come to the elements of social morality and practice? It was at first also much less important what idea was formed of the nature of the gods, rather than that the social groups should feel themselves combined through the honouring of certain higher powers, and that they should have in this common consciousness of a higher obligation a regulating principle of their common life with each other. But after social customs and ordinances had settled themselves under the influence of this religious motive, and certain fundamental conceptions of right and wrong had been developed, it was then natural that they should see in the Deity the Guardian of the social order willed by him, and consequently the avenger of every wrong, including civil crimes, and not merely the religious trespass in the narrower sense. But when the gods came to be regarded as the representatives and guardians of the sacred order of justice, the further consequence could not but follow that a corresponding sentiment should be attributed to them, and that they should be thought of as friends, promoters, and examples of all that was regarded by their worshippers as good and noble. Thus was formed the conception of the gods as moral ideals, and this conception again reacted upon the moral consciousness out of which it had grown so as to strengthen it. There was therefore found from the beginning a relationship of closest reciprocity between the religious and the moral; and the development of the two sides proceeded for a long time *pari passu*, and under the reciprocal influence of the one upon the other.

In the course of time, however, this immediate unity of religion and morality must necessarily become looser and be dissolved. A conservative characteristic belongs to religion; it clings to the traditional which is held by it as sacred and revealed by the Deity. Morality, on the other hand, advances unceasingly forwards; its circles widen; the wants of life become more numerous; with the advancing division of labour society becomes organised more distinguishably, the contrast of the different classes becomes greater; and the legal relationships become more complicated. Then the old morals and dogmas transmitted under religious sanctions no longer apply; they are found to be adverse to their purpose, and to be a hindrance to the rational order of society. The sceptical understanding assumes an attitude of opposition to their supposed origin in divine revelation when it comes to reflect upon the difference between the manners and laws of the several peoples, and from this it draws the inference of their human origin. Thus a breach arises between the traditional religion of the people and the moral consciousness, first in the case of individuals, and then gradually of whole generations. The moral thus loosens itself from the religious foundation which it had at first, and seeks an autonomous grounding for itself in human nature. So it was among the Greeks in the time of the Sophists, who declared man to be the measure of all things; and so it was again in the modern period of rationalistic enlightenment — the period of the *Aufklärung*.

But before we pursue the different forms of religionless morality, and examine their tenableness, let us still pause for a moment to consider religious morality, and notice the defects which result from its immediate dependence on the sanction of positive religious authorities. We find the classical examples for this point of view in the Judaism of the period after the Exile, and in the Catholicism of the Middle Ages. In such cases the moral subject continually remains under the guardianship of priestly authority, and no progress is made beyond the irresponsible conditions of childhood to a proper moral conviction and free personal sentiments. The good is not known as what it is in itself, as the true end of our own will; but it appears as the groundless arbitrary requirement of an external will, of the God who has proclaimed His law through His ambassadors, and who has impressed its fulfilment by the threatenings of punishment and the promises of reward. That the motives corresponding to this view—namely, fear of divine punishment and hope of divine reward— only produce a lower slavish morality, has been often and rightly observed: but, in addition to this, it is to be observed that, upon this standpoint, an essential understanding of the good according to its rational purposive relation to the wellbeing of man is not possible; and hence, that all moral laws are only to be accepted on external authority. From this there results a manifold train of evils. Morality is resolved into a sum of positive commands and prohibitions which refer to individual actions or omissions; and everything depends upon these commandments being punctually observed, without distinction, for they have all the same divine sanction. Thereby morality obtains that external formalistic and petty pedantic character, such as we know it in Phariseeism, which strains out gnats and swallows camels. Further, the legislation that rests upon religious tradition always requires authorised expounders, scribes, and priests, who have to apply the laws fixed in the sacred letter to the manifold individual cases of conduct, and to define it more exactly. Now, as these representatives of religious authority are accustomed only too easily to confound the interests of their class with the divine will, there arises from this a spurious falsification of the moral values of things by performances for the Church and the Priesthood being placed above the fulfilment of the nearest moral duties. "Howbeit in vain do they worship me, teaching for doctrines the commandments of men" (Mark vii. 7), is the reproach addressed by Jesus to the Pharisees. The medieval Church, by its ascetic contempt of the world, especially degraded the moral orders that are grounded in the nature of humanity, such as the family, the work of one's calling, and the national State, declaring them to be not only worthless, but even hindrances to the eternal salvation of men; and it exalted self-mortification and obedience to the Church as the truly meritorious mode of action. Thus, by the so-called "supernatural" morality demanded by the Church, the true natural moral order of the world was repressed and distorted.

Against this unnaturalness, this compulsion of priestly guardianship, the sound moral sense of man rightly rebelled: it would not continue to be a mere child guided by the leading-strings of authority, but strove to attain to the free self-determination of the man. And in this connection it happened quite naturally that in the struggle against the slavish religious morality of the Church, it was thought that a free morality could only be found by tearing one's self away from all religion— nay, in opposition to all religion. This was natural, for extremes meet; and, as has been well said—

> "Fear well the slave whene'er he breaks his chain,
> But aye before the freeman fear is vain."

Is there not something of the passionate bitterness of the slave struggling for his freedom to be heard even in the judgments of many of our contemporaries regarding the emancipation of morality? This question I would here raise at least for preliminary consideration. Before we attempt to answer it, we have to subject to examination the forms and principles in which a religionless secular morality has grounded and fashioned itself.

In antiquity and in modern times there are found in this connection essentially two chief tendencies which we must distinguish, and which we may designate as the empirical or eudæmonistic, and the idealistic or rationalistic. As the Greek Cyrenaics and Epicureans, so the modern Utilitarians have started again from the proposition, which is accepted by them as an indubitable axiom, that the fundamental impulse of man is the striving after pleasure, and that from this impulse all morality must be deduced. They teach that that is good which helps man to the greatest possible and lasting pleasure. From regard to lasting pleasure or happiness, momentary pleasure must often be sacrificed. And, because the individual is so closely connected with others that their weal and woe also condition his weal and woe, every one cares best for his own happiness if he also gives the greatest possible consideration to the requirement of the happiness of others. Hence the famous formula, that the highest moral principle is the greatest possible happiness of the greatest possible number of men.

In considering this theory, we remark, in the first place, that a psychological error underlies it. From the fact that pleasure is constantly the result of the happy activity of our impulses, the Hedonist wrongly concludes that pleasure is also always the cause of our impulses, and the only supreme motive. As pleasure is the indication of the satisfied impulse, the existence and working of an impulse must always be presupposed before there can be any question of pleasure or non-pleasure. It is not the reflection upon the pleasurable result which may be expected that impels us to action, but simply the unreflected pressure of some one of the manifold impulses implanted in our nature. But if pleasure is the feeling resulting from the activity of the impulses, then the more precise quality of the average lasting feeling of pleasure or happiness in the case of every man, depends on what impulses or tendencies of the will are predominating and ruling in him. As different as men are in temperament, course of life, culture, and character, so different becomes their taste for what lastingly produces weal or woe, and so different therefore will be their ideal of happiness. But then, how is it possible to establish what the general happiness, or the greatest possible happiness of the greatest possible number, consists in? Shall we set about arranging some universal way of voting upon the subject, and get every one at the poll, man by man, to declare in what he considers his highest happiness to lie? I fear the result of this universal *enquête* would be of such a kind that all true friends of the people would keep from recognising it as the canon of their philanthropic efforts. And does not this involve the clear proof that "happiness" is a much too indefinite and undefinable conception for being fitted to be the supreme principle of morality?

A further important consideration arises as a second objection to this theory. As pleasure and happiness are a matter of subjective feeling, the striving of the *individual* after happiness must necessarily form the basis of the eudæmonistic ethics. But on what ground is the individual to be required to strive after the happiness of others and even of all? This question is the Achilles-heel of Utilitarianism. The representatives of this theory indeed are wont to satisfy themselves very easily on this point by assuming at once that the universal happiness includes that of all individuals, and therefore that every one, in caring for the happiness of others, *eo ipso*, cares likewise best for his own. But things are not actually so simple as this. Experience much rather shows that the wellbeing of others, of society, of a people, often enough does not coincide with that of the individual, but crosses it; and that such wellbeing demands sacrifices of individual happiness, renunciation of one's own advantage and personal comfort, and even under certain circumstances the very life of the individual. What then is to determine a man from the utilitarian standpoint to such a self-denying altruistic mode of action? Such conduct cannot, at all events, be derived as a duty from the supreme principle of individual happiness: on the contrary, one would think that self-denial in favour of others must be judged to be immoral, being in contradiction with the supreme moral principle. The utilitarians are indeed seldom resolute enough to draw this consequence. Rather do they seek to escape from the difficulty by referring to the many artificial motives by which society seeks to impel individuals to a common useful mode of conduct, and to restrain them from actions that would be prejudicial to the community. Such motives are fear of civil punishment, or of the disapprobation of public opinion, or of shame and disgrace on the one hand, and on the other hand, hope of the esteem of society, of honour and reputation, or even of an untarnished name, and of the manifold advantages which arise to the individual from the secured existence of the public legalised order. And who would deny that such motives are, at all events, not to be underestimated in their significance as *co-operating factors* of the moral life? The question is only whether they are also adequate when taken as the *sole* basis and supreme principle of morals? I believe that this must be denied on several grounds. In the first place, it is to be denied because all the motives derived from the external consequences of actions can be determining only for the external conduct, and not for the inner sentiment of the actor. Morality, however, in distinction from legal right, has to do with this inner sentiment. Whether any one restrains himself from what is bad from fear of civil punishment and public disgrace, or from an aversion to what is mean and unworthy of him, makes no difference, when judged from the utilitarian consideration of the result of his act; and yet the alternative is very different for the moral judgment. This characteristic of the moral judgment, that it is directed not merely to the actions but to the motives and sentiment of the actor, cannot find any ground in utilitarianism; and hence, in any case, it could not be fitted to be the supreme principle of morals, but in the most favourable case only to be the principle of a legal order. But more exactly viewed, it is not sufficient even for this. For, if it is only by consideration of the consequences of his action as useful or prejudicial to him that the individual man lets himself be determined, one cannot conceive what should restrain him whenever he has not to fear any, or comparatively trivial, evil consequences, from pursuing his own advantage in the most unscrupulous way, at the cost of his fellow-men. The prudent egoist who, without getting into collision with the penal law and preservation of his external position, knows how he can mercilessly make use of others as instruments and sacrifices for his own advantage—nay, even the prudent criminal, who may understand how to keep himself free from punishment—would not be to blame from the standpoint of a prudent calculation of utility. But it is clear that, in a society in which such a way of thinking was universally prevalent, the legal order could not permanently exist, but would necessarily soon be dissolved into the chaos of a "*bellum omnium contra omnes."* The historical example of this issue is presented in the history of French society at the end of the last century.

Finally, if the Eudæmonists, along with the external consequences of actions, also reflect upon their inner consequences, such as the joy of a good conscience and of self-esteem, the pain of a bad conscience and of self-contempt, and would derive from them efficient motives, they are thus manifestly borrowing from the idealistic moral principle, otherwise combated by them. They must, however, first show how such moral feelings are at all possible from their eudæmonistic standpoint. Certain as it is that the man in whom the feeling of duty lives, shrinks from evil as a source of inner misery, just as little can this feeling, which already presupposes the consciousness of the obligatory authority of the good, be made the ground of this very consciousness, or the principle of morality. If a man be once told that the striving after happiness is the supreme determining principle of action, he cannot be prevented from seeking his happiness in the satisfaction of *those* impulses which he finds to be the strongest. If these happen to be the sensuous and selfish impulses, he may then indeed be pitied on account of his bad taste, but he cannot be blamed for his violation of the moral principle. Nor will much be effected in his case by warning him against the evil consequences of his mode of action, or the pain of an evil conscience and of self-contempt, for appeal is then made to feelings which have not been developed in the course of his striving after happiness, and towards which he holds himself indifferent, nay, which he even repudiates with proud contempt, because they could only prevent him from seeking and enjoying the happiness of life in *his* own way. We cannot gather grapes from thorns. If subjective eudæmonism is taken as the principle of morality, no dialectical art will ever succeed in deriving from it the unconditioned authority of the good, independent of the inclination and favour of the individual, or the sanctity of duty. And wherever this appears to be the case, there is always involved a *petitio principii*. The feeling of duty, the founding of which is here in question, is already silently assumed as present, and it is then certainly easy to show how, in judging of the relative value of individual modes of action, their consequences are regulated for human wellbeing. However justified utilitarianism may be as a heuristic principle in the process of valuing individual actions, it is as little available as a foundation for moral sentiment and the formation of character.

This has been well recognised by the idealistic moralists from Zeno to Kant, and they have therefore sought for the foundation of autonomous morality in an opposite way. According to the Stoics, the virtue, dignity, and happiness of man consist not in the satisfaction of the desires, but in freedom from desires, in apathy, or in the supremacy of the passionless reason. And Kant in like manner taught again that our reason unconditionally commands us to respect the dignity of humanity in every man, to recognise every person as a subject of rights and duties, and always to fulfil our own duty unconditionally, purely from respect for duty, independent of all inclination, and even in constant conflict with inclination. Certainly there is something sublime in this Kantian view of virtue which belongs unconditionally to duty, from pure respect for the law, or for our own reason as the lawgiver, and which concedes no rights whatever to the inclinations, but on the contrary proves its higher descent and strength just in conflict with them. But it may well be asked, Is this sublime virtue not cold, and even repellently cold, when it appeals to us? Was Schiller not right when he said that this morality of the categorical imperative "is a morality for slaves, and one which the children of the house do not deserve"? and was the Gospel not right when it showed us in heartfelt love to the divine ideal of the good, a higher, because freer and gladder, morality than that of the law?

But if we ask how this rigorism of the Kantian ethics, which reminds us of the Stoa, is explained, we shall recognise the same ground for it as in the case of Stoicism. It lies in the ascetic dualism which severs reason from nature, and in the rigid individualism which severs the individual from the fellowship of mankind and of the Deity. In order to secure the dignity of man as a moral personality, Kant believed that it was necessary to set him entirely upon himself, upon his own reason and autonomous freedom, and to exclude him from all the influences of nature, and of human society, and God. He resolved the moral world into a plurality of spiritual monads, between which there is found no moral reciprocity, no bond of solidarity of its members, no organic development of the common spirit, no divine education of the whole. But how under such a presupposition can we find it thinkable that the weak voice of the law-giving reason of the individual could ever procure for itself hearing and respect from the sensuous and selfish impulses which are only continually resisting it? In fact, such an abstract reason would never be able to realise its moral demand; humanity would never be able to come even to the first steps of moral development were there not already implanted in our nature those social impulses and feelings which bind the individual from the beginning instinctively to the community, and which, developed by the educating influence of society, become powers for good, in which the later awakening voice of the law-giving reason finds its inner natural representative and echo. Kant, by ignoring this natural connection of the individual with the species, not only made the growth of the good and the realisation of reason in man inconceivable, but he also evacuated the idea of the good of all determinate contents. In place of the manifold moral goods which the divine-human spirit has created in history, and which can become to the heart of man an object of reverence, devotion, love, and inspiration, Kant has put the empty formula of duty, which repels the feeling heart, suppresses the living individuality, and makes the moral world stiffen into barren monotony.

It is not wonderful that a protest was raised against this suppression of individual feelings, even by such men as otherwise gave their full approval to the idealism of the Kantian ethics. The Herders and Schillers, the Fichtes and Schleiermachers, were not less averse to the ordinary utilitarian morality than Kant; but, on the other hand, they could not be satisfied with the irreconcilable discordance asserted by Kant between reason and nature, duty and inclination; they were convinced that this opposition must find its reconciliation in a higher morality, in which duty itself has become the object of inclination, the good has become the good that yields happiness, and obligation has become the free and joyous volition of the will. They designated this higher moral ideal by various names—they called it humanity, moral beauty, freedom, love; but they were always agreed in holding that it is what is properly divine in man, what raises him above the narrow limit of his own selfhood, and unites him with the primary source of spirits. Thus, by carrying idealism itself to a deeper position, they at last reached a religious morality which, however far it might be removed from the ecclesiastical faith of revelation and authority, yet came into closest contact with the fundamental character of Christian morality. Nor did these original thinkers at the beginning of this century deny the connection of their ethical idealism with Christianity: with all their free attitude towards the Church and dogma, they had yet so much historical sense as to recognise that the humanity, the beautiful culture, and the love in which they beheld the moral ideal, was a fruit that had ripened on the tree of Christianity. It was the Epigons about the middle of this century, such as Feuerbach in Germany, the two Mills in England, and Comte in France, who first began to accentuate the difference of their free secular morality from that of Christianity, and to carry it out to a sharp, extreme contrast. Since that time it appears almost to be regarded as if it belonged to good tone in the circles of advanced culture to boast of the independence of morality from all and every religion, as the highest achievement of the present time. This position seems to recall in many respects the old history of the friendship between Pilate and Herod. Representatives of the opposite tendencies, namely, idealists and utilitarians, are now seen uniting with each other and working together in union for the spread of an emancipated secular religionless morality.

What are we to say, then, regarding this phenomenon? In the first place, we may regard it as a natural product of our time, when extremes are everywhere carried out to the sharpest opposition. In particular, the striving of the different Churches for power and supremacy now makes itself everywhere felt in increased energy, and opposes to all the struggling of the new time for a reform of the traditional doctrines and dogmas only a rigid *non possumus*, and exhorts us modern men to bring to it the sacrifice of intellect. This naturally incites the self-conscious spirits of the age to haughty opposition, and drives them into the arms of a Voltairean radicalism, which believes that it can find moral progress only by a breach in principle with religion and the Church. But however conceivable this mood of many of our contemporaries may be, yet it cannot be regarded as sound or wholesome. We indeed willingly admit that to-day, as in all former times, there are many estimable moral characters among the irreligious men of our time—men who are distinguished by strict conscientiousness, faithful fulfilment of the duties of their calling, and devoted zeal for the wellbeing of their fellow-men; but, far as I am from wishing to dispute this experience, I would still raise a warning against drawing too rashly from such isolated examples of religionless morality universal conclusions regarding the normal relationship of religion and morality.

I should like, in the first place, to refer to the fact that the moral principles and sentiments of such men have nevertheless not become what they are of themselves, but are the fruit of their education by the Christian community, which led the young by doctrine and example to the recognition of the good as what is absolutely valuable, as a "sacred" authority, and which deeply impressed on their still susceptible hearts the feelings of reverence and piety, and of obligation and love for the ideals of the good. To the subsequent influence of this education by the Christian community, whether they are conscious of it or not, we owe the best of our moral convictions and the formation of our character. But it is at the same time an unquestionable fact that the Christian community rests on a religious foundation, and that its moral sentiment is rooted in its religious belief. The good is regarded by it as the absolute authority, not because it is useful, but because it is the revelation of the holy will of God; its faith in the victory of the good in the world rests not upon the postulate of the subjective reason, but upon the objective experiences of history, in which it recognises revelations of the judging and saving, the redeeming and educating, spirit of God. This radical implication of morality in the religious view of the world and history may indeed pass from the consciousness of particular individuals who have been educated by the Christian community, but it continues to exist in the common spirit of the whole community, by which the individual moral spirit is maintained and reared. Now, if we put the case that the religious faith which has hitherto formed the root of the moral convictions in Christian society has fallen away, not merely in the case of individual persons, but for whole generations, would it then be probable that the moral convictions could thereafter also assert themselves without modification in the purity and power with which they have been hitherto propagated by the Christian training? The experience of history does not appear to speak for its being so; rather does it show that, in times of religious decay, general languidness of faith, and scepticism, the moral consciousness is also wont to sink, and fall into weakness, confusion, and dissolution.

I should like further to raise the question whether in the case of many and even the most earnest representatives of religionless morality, the professed irreligiosity is not rather more apparent than real? They repudiate the religion exhibited in the definite form of the ecclesiastical dogmas in which they have learned to know it; but does it follow from this that religious belief, or piety, is extraneous to them in every sense? In the case of men of truly moral sentiment we may well doubt the possibility of their total irreligiousness; for the upright man who is earnestly interested not merely in the appearance of the good or external legality and respectability, but for the good itself, cannot but attribute to the good the highest right in the world, and therefore must demand its victorious assertion and accomplishment in reality. But in demanding this, and feeling the right of this demand, he will also have the courage to believe in its truth, to believe therefore in the good as the true power over the world, or in such a constitution of the actual world that it must serve as a means for the realisation of the good. Now this belief in "the moral world-order" is in fact already "religion"; it is the religion of Fichte, of Matthew Arnold, and of many ethical idealists. Whether religious belief could not, and should not, be still more definitely apprehended, is a question of second rank, which will engage our attention in a later connection. We may here, however, recall the fact that Fichte soon advanced from belief in the moral world-order to faith in God as the sole principle of all that is true and good. And it is in truth a near consequence that the good, if it is the *end* of the world, must likewise be its *ground;* and if it is both the ground and end of the world, it must likewise rule the *whole* course of the world, and consequently reveal itself not only in the far future, but in the whole historical reality as the spiritual power that progressively realises itself. In recognising this we stand, as a matter of fact, upon the basis of the

Christian faith in God, as has also been distinctly recognised by Fichte in his later philosophy of religion.

Where the moral consciousness is not able to rise to this faith, and to find in it its immovable foundation, it is always threatened with the danger of losing its energy in conflict with empirical reality, and ultimately becoming perplexed. One can only deceive one's self regarding this danger so long as the eyes are closed in naïve optimism to the power of the evil and badness that are in the world outside of us, and to the weakness of one's own heart, as is indeed the case at the moment with most of the heralds of the religion of humanity or of religionless morality. But experience also teaches that this simple optimism is not able to stand long before the harsh power of reality. There is certainly something great in universal philanthropy, that principle of Christian morality; but if it is no longer, as in Christianity, the fruit of religious belief, but a substitute for it, then the serious question arises whether men as they exhibit themselves in experience are really so amiable that it would be an easy thing to love them unceasingly, to exert all one's powers for their good, and to make the greatest sacrifices for them? If the philanthropist is rewarded with bitter ingratitude when his noblest endeavours fail, from the callousness of some and the malice of others, must not his enthusiasm be chilled, and his courage in sacrifice and action be maimed, unless he draw unconquerable force from his faith in the power of a goodness which overcomes the world as it appears, and is therefore divine? He only can love men in a lasting and energetic way who looks not merely upon what is before his eyes, namely, the common reality, but who believes in the indestructible divine element in man; but how can one believe on the divine *in* man without belief in the divine which is *superior* and *prior* to man, the eternal spirit, of whom and through whom and to whom are all things? It is undoubtedly possible that even where the wings of philanthropic enthusiasm have been broken by rough contact with reality, the feeling of duty may still remain strong enough to determine permanently the moral guidance of life. Experience shows us not seldom such stoical characters, who, without loving men, and even with expressed contempt of them, yet keep firm and unmoved to duty for the sake of duty. Undisturbed by the success or failure of their actions, they hold fast to what they know to be right as that which is commanded by their reason. They respect the law of their reason, because they must otherwise lose respect for themselves. Such virtue we must always regard as estimable: we may well admire its power of defying the world, but we will hardly trust its power to overcome the world. The very hardness which it uses to protect and steel itself against the world, slays those tenderer feelings which bind man to the world, and open to him the entrance to the hearts of his fellow-men. The rough severity of this virtue does not exercise a warming and attracting, but a repelling and chilling, influence upon its surroundings; it isolates the moral person from society, and thereby cuts off his moral influence upon it; and the feeling of this isolation engenders but too easily a pessimistic bitterness and proud haughtiness towards the despised crowd. This is the frequent fate of those strong natures who, for the humble and trustful morality of the pious soul, would substitute the proud morality of the autonomous law of reason. But for weak natures it is altogether to be feared that respect for the autonomous moral law would be but an inadequate substitute for the religious support of the moral consciousness in its struggle with the adversities and temptations of life. Belief in determinate dogmas may certainly disappear without any injury to morality, seeing that they are only artificial and fallible attempts to interpret man's religious experience; but where the kernel of religious faith has also disappeared — namely, the conviction that the world is God's, and that the course of the world is subservient to the realisation of the divine purpose of good,—what could then give the moral consciousness power to protect itself from sceptical dissolution? If the good is not the governing power of the *world*, why should *I* then still recognise it as the authority binding on my will? If I find myself in a world in which nothing is found but selfishness sporting in a hundred forms and disguises, and victoriously achieving its ends, why then should I be an exception to others, and sacrifice my inclinations and interests to what I have been taught to regard as my duty? What then—so at last asks the sceptical understanding—what then gives duty the higher right as superior to my inclinations? If it be only my own thought, why should I not then be also the lord over my own thoughts? If it is a rule of action which I have set to myself from my own freedom, why then should I not be able again to loosen myself from this rule when it becomes too inconvenient for me? But if it is a rule which others have devised and prescribed to me, what then obliges me to give obedience to the will of others who are not more than I am, and who also only follow after their selfish interests? If selfishness stands opposed to selfishness, why should my self-seeking not have just as much right as that of others? Am I not the nearest one to myself? Have not I therefore the right to make myself, my own wishes and interests, the measure of all things, the criterion of all my actions?

It would be difficult to say how the moral consciousness could preserve itself from such sceptical dissolution if it wholly severed itself from all religious foundation. The moral law will only be able to assert its absolute validity if it springs not out of the thinking of individual men, whether it be my thinking or that of others, but is the revelation of the willing of the universal reason, which stands *above* all individual wills as their ground, and is at the same time active *in* them as the common bond of their community. This is just the divine will. In so far as all individuals feel themselves bound to this power which rules over the whole, they are also bound internally to each other; and, indeed, bound by a bond which rests in the ground of their being, and which consequently precedes all particular desire and choice and reflection, which is not a product of their freedom, but the presupposition, and therefore the power, the authority, over their freedom. But in this transcendental obligation of all, there is likewise contained, together with duty, the right of every person to be recognised and esteemed by others as a rational being and an end in himself. Resting upon the ground of the divine will, human society is a moral organism in which all stand for one, and one for all. Take that religious ground away, and society dissolves into a chaos, in which every one is against all, and all against every one.

If I may now attempt to sum up the result of what has been said, it appears to me that the relation of religion and morality may be most simply determined in this way. They have both a common root, which is the transcendental fact of the human will being bound to the universal or divine will; but this principle obtains immediate manifestation in religion as the union of God and man, while in morality it appears mediately as the social bond of the individual and society. So far it may be said that religion contains the ideal ground of morality, and morality the real manifestation of religion. From this it follows that each of them has its truth only in union with the other; and, on the other hand, that either of them must become stunted and falsified when torn away from the other. If religion tears itself away from morality, then its symbolical representation of the transcendental principle of unity becomes an empty form, a mere image, mythology and ceremonial worship; and in so far as a mysterious truth and power are still ascribed to these empty forms, to these fantastic ideas and arbitrary ceremonies, then religion, robbed of its moral content, becomes perverted into a caricature of the truth, and from this proceed pernicious superstition, magic, and fanaticism—religious malformations or deformities by which the moral life of individuals and of the community is injured and suppressed. Against this the moral spirit then reacts by tearing itself away from religion, and by seeking to quieten itself upon an extra-religious secular basis. In this lies indeed a step of progress, in so far as morality, freed from the hindrances put in its way by the superstitious and hierarchical ordinances of positive religion, then gains independence of movement, which enables it to order society according to the natural wants and rational ends of human nature. But if, with the statutory coverings of religion, there is given up at the same time its essential kernel, which contains the ideal principle of morality itself, the result is that the secularised morality becomes stunted and dies, like the plant which has been cut off from its roots. Then in place of the genuine moral sentiment, there comes the surrogate of an egoistic prudential morality, or even the naturalism of a war of all against all, the disorganisation of society, which leads to a universal unfreedom. True, the idealistic morality strives after something higher, by the attempt to ground morality upon the autonomous reason; but by isolating this principle in the thinking subject and separating it from the historical life of the community, it falls into an unfruitful formalism, which is not able to take the place of the religious root of morality. Accordingly, experience shows that morality can just as little flourish without religion as religion without morality; while religion sinks into pseudo-religious superstition and fanaticism, morality sinks into a pseudo-moral naturalism and abstract formalism. Hence it follows that, as they both spring out of the same root, so they can only develop normally into full harmony and living reciprocity with each other.

It is the great and eternal truth of *Christianity* that it has raised this inner connection of religion and morality to a principle. Morality has here its firm ground, its living root, in the consciousness of our sonship to God, in love to God the Father, and to Christ, the ideal of the divine Man, and in surrender to the universal divine purpose of the world—namely, the kingdom of God, that ideal of the perfect community and fellowship of humanity, which is not a mere ideal, an abstract postulate and problem of human striving, but is always at the same time a growing reality, a working of the divine spirit in historical humanity, and which therefore also contains the real possibility and guarantee for the becoming good and blessed of all the individuals who surrender themselves to this spirit as its instrument. And as the Christian morality has its firm ground in faith in God and the coming of the kingdom of God, so, on the other hand, the Christian religion has its real manifestation in morality. "This is the love of God, that we keep His commandments." "And this commandment have we from Him, That he who loveth God love his brother also." Jesus has connected love to man with love to God as the same great commandment, and Paul has called love fulfilment of the law. Not in lip-service that says "Lord, Lord," and not in the practice of ceremonial worship, but in the rational worship (Romans xii. 2) of the moral life, does Christian piety find its manifestation and authentication. Christianity is not faith merely, and not charity alone, but "faith, hope, charity, these three; but the greatest of these is charity."

LECTURE III.

RELIGION AND SCIENCE.

As with the beginnings of morals, the beginnings of science among all peoples likewise lie in religion. Myths and legends are the original forms in which man's impulse to find his place in the world sought to satisfy itself; and out of them proceeded the cosmologies which everywhere form the beginnings of a philosophical explanation of the world. But as secular morality with the progress of civilisation separated itself from religion, so in like manner the impulse towards knowledge did not feel itself permanently satisfied by the traditional legends. Men sought by independent reflection on the phenomena around them for better answers as to the *What* and *Whence* of things, and in this way they soon came to hypotheses and views which stood in more or less manifest opposition to the religious traditions. Our own age feels more painfully than any former time has done the pressure of the opposition between faith and knowledge; and this is proved by the ever-renewed attempts to reach in one way or another a solution of this opposition, or at least to bring about a mitigation of the extreme tension now holding between religion and science.

Let us, in the first place, survey the relation of religion and science in its historical development, and then try to discover in the nature of the cognitive mind the point of contact with religion, and consequently the connecting point for a mediation between religion and science.

A theoretical factor is essential to all religion; man must form an idea of the power that governs his world, and of his own position in relation to it and to the world. But its interest does not turn upon an exact knowledge of the individual in detail, such as the understanding seeks to obtain by observation and comparison, abstraction and combination; on the contrary, the organ of knowledge involved in religion is originally only the *fantasy* which objectifies religious feelings in images of sensible perception, and thus creates myths, fables, and legends. Mythology is the natural language of religion, the indispensable investment of spiritual emotions and aspirations in sensible images. But this investment is effected so unconsciously and involuntarily that no distinction is made between the spiritual content and the sensible form. The sensible object, whether it be a natural phenomenon or man, which awakens in the soul the religious impression of a higher world of spiritual mysterious powers, is so identified with this impression that it appears itself immediately as the divine. Thus arise the primitive religious myths in which content and form are still immediately one, and the spiritual is present in the consciousness only in and with the sensible. In the further spinning out of the legends there undoubtedly also works the free creative fantasy, whose end is æsthetic enjoyment, and which plays freely with its forms in the interest of poetic beauty. But from this artistic creation of the epic poets the original religious mythical creation is distinguished in the soul of the people in this, that in the latter case the fantasy does not yet stand as a free superior over its object, nor does it deal freely with its forms, but is still so wrapped up in its objects that it believes in its own forms.

Even in the higher religions, in which the divine is no longer identified with the phenomena of nature, but is known as a higher object above nature, the religious spirit still requires the creative fantasy in order to give to its inner experiences a sensible expression. From this need spring those *miraculous legends*, in which historical processes become idealised into images and types of spiritual experiences which always repeat themselves in the life of pious souls, or in which super-sensible truths, ideas, and ideals, sprung from the inner world of the spirit, become realised in symbolical processes of the external world. In order to know the good as the true, the human mind requires a mediation of the two by poetic beauty, in which the idea comes to manifestation in the medium of the real, and in which the sensible is transfigured so as to become the transparent veil of the spiritual. This combination of spiritual significance and sensible expression is thus always characteristic of the religious mode of representation: the whole language of the Bible bears witness to it. And so long as this mode of speech finds naïve religious apprehension, the sensible form does not make itself felt as in any way disturbing the spiritual meaning. It is not till the reflecting understanding comes in and seeks to understand literally what is meant figuratively, and when it would fix the indefinite flowing and ever-changing representations into fixed conceptions and doctrines, that the difficulties, the absurdities, and the contradictions arise which demand solution, explanation, and mediation. This was the task of the Fathers of the Christian Church from the end of the second century on through several centuries. In order to repel the errors of the heretics, and to grasp the faith of the Church in fixed, universally authoritative propositions or "dogmas," they made use of the Greek philosophy as in their time the universally employed medium of didactic communication and elucidation. This procedure was the more readily adopted, seeing that Plato's transcendent world of ideas came closely into touch with the transcendent kingdom of heaven of the Christian Apocalypse, and as the notion of the Logos in the Hellenistic philosophy had already been employed in the New Testament to designate the revelation of God in Jesus Christ. It would undoubtedly be doing wrong to the Church Fathers if the intention were ascribed to them of transforming the Christian religion into philosophy, or making philosophy a substitute for it: rather did they accept the religious faith of the Church as the established basis upon which the scientific theologian had to place himself in order to unfold the contents of the religious consciousness by the aid of philosophy, to understand one particular in connection with another, and thus to gain a better view of the sense and meaning of the whole. Nevertheless, it cannot be denied that, in consequence of the dogmatic controversies, the original religious meaning of the ecclesiastical doctrines always retreated more behind the formulas artificially constructed out of the philosophical and juristic conceptions of the schools. Still more does this hold true of Scholasticism. With the production of the dogmas, the understanding of their religious motives had also disappeared; only the petrified product had remained —namely, the rigid formulas of the decrees of the Councils, which were honoured the more as sacred relics the more their incomprehensibility appeared to point to a higher origin. This ecclesiastical authority was further supplemented in the twelfth century by that of the Aristotelian philosophy, the knowledge of which had been learned through the medium of the Arabs. In the double slavery under these so entirely heterogeneous two authorities, and in the despairing effort to be equally just to both, the scientific power of the Middle Ages consumed itself. Faith, corrupted by the false knowledge of the scholastics, let no genuine knowledge arise; and it held the mind that was thirsting for knowledge in such hard chains that it finally despaired of even being able to know anything. The scholastic theology, which aimed at rearing up a universal science on the basis of authority, ended in scepticism. The mixture of Biblical religion and Greco-Roman science, which was what the Christian theology had been through all the centuries of the patristic and scholastic periods, however useful it might have been as an educational means for educating the peoples still in their pupilage, became at last an intolerable fetter for faith as well as for knowledge.

The way for the dissolution of this false, because unfree, unity of religion and science was paved on both sides by the reform of faith which proceeded from Mysticism, and by the liberation of science which proceeded from the renascence of antiquity. This mysticism, which in the later Middle Ages passed into more and more decided opposition to scholasticism, laid the dogmas and their dialectical dissection aside, and reflected immediately upon the object itself—that is, on the inner religious experience of the pious soul, its unblessedness in separation from God, and its blissfulness in humble, trustful surrender to Him. If there often arose an ascetic tendency from this mystic piety, yet it was always characterised by its inner feeling of the love of God, and by a high moral earnestness; and out of the depth of this religious experience there proceeded in the case of individual thinkers (like Meister Eckart) an original theological speculation, which was far removed from the dogmatism of the school, and which was typical for the future. It is well known how closely the Reformation of the sixteenth century was connected with the pre-Reformation mysticism. Luther was himself an admirer of the "German Theology," which sprang from the school of Eckart. The Protestant mystics attached themselves immediately to their spiritual kinsmen of the pre-Reformation period, and although they were expelled from the official Churches of the Reformation, they yet preserved the genuine spirit of the Reformation in many respects more purely than these Churches themselves. But the ecclesiastical theology of Protestantism, from the need of a didactically developed system of faith, returned again to the old dogmas; and thus there soon again arose a new scholasticism, which at least equalled the old scholasticism in its want of freedom and in its dry formalism.

Yet these partially retrograde currents could not keep back the new advance of non-theological secular science which had proceeded from the impetus of the Renaissance. While the theologians were still busily employed in the Churches in restoring the old dogmas which had been drawn up on the basis of the Ptolemaic cosmology, and which fitted only into its framework, this cosmology was destroyed by Copernicus and supplanted by the new view of the world which stands in utter contradiction to the whole of the system of the ecclesiastical dogmatics from the Creation to the coming down of Christ from heaven and His return again, as was clearly recognised by Melanchthon much more acutely than by all his later followers. As Astronomy attained to a knowledge of the laws of the motions of the heavenly bodies, so did physics and mechanics investigate the laws of the terrestrial world, and mathematics furnished the most general and precise formulæ for the results of observation and experiment. From the natural sciences and mathematics there was thus formed the conception of the conformity of all that happens in the world to law. Men began to view "Nature" as an ordered whole, in which all particular being and happening are conditioned by their causal connection with everything else by immutable laws. Spinoza gave this thought the philosophical foundation and construction by which it became the principle of that universal view of the world which extends far beyond the investigation of nature, which has been designated by the name of enlightenment or illuminism (*Aufklärung*), and which is essentially homogeneous with the "positivism" of the present day. How far this intellectual view, which would conceive and explain everything in the world according to the law of causality, lay from the poetic mythological view, to which miracles, and the interferences of higher beings with the course of things, had been things natural and self-evident! This self-intelligibility of the supernatural and miraculous, which was still regarded as indubitable by the thinkers of the middle ages and of the period of the Reformation, was no longer possible from the time of the eighteenth century. In the world of experience with which science has to do, there could be no more holding of miracles as events which were not to be explained by the orderly causal connection of things in space and time. The attempt was therefore first made to limit miracles to rare exceptional cases in the far past, which were to be believed on the ground of the tradition of sacred history. But what if this support of them also became problematical? And in fact there sprang up a second opponent to orthodoxy, and not the least dangerous one, in *historical investigation*. The principle of the necessary connection of causes and effects being also applied to the historical life of man, there arose the "pragmatic method," which sought to explain historical events everywhere from the concurrence of individual circumstances and motives, and put in place of the intentions of Providence the intentions of the acting man and the play of accident. Moreover, in the school of humanistic science students had now grown accustomed to careful investigation of sources, and to criticism of the documents handed down from the past. The application of this method to the sources of Biblical and ecclesiastical history led to the beginnings of Biblical criticism, which, modest as they were at the outset, yet proved more and more sufficient to shatter the foundation of the orthodox dogmas, the inspiration of the Bible. Thus from all sides there accumulated doubts of the possibility and reality of the supernatural and miraculous as such, not merely in the experience of the present, but also in the past of which the sacred history treated.

What was to become of faith in presence of this enlightened knowledge? How was the divine still to find a place in a world where all goes on naturally, where everything is the regular effect of finite causes? Various attempts have been made to mitigate by reasonable compromises the tension of this antagonism, which has been occupying the thinking of the Christian world for now about two centuries. Such a compromise is presented in the *supra-naturalism* that proceeded from the Leibnitz-Wolffian school, which accepts the view of the world taken by the *Aufklärung* in general with regard to our religious experience, and limits miracles to individual exceptional cases, in which the order of nature is broken through by supernatural omnipotence for the sake of higher ends. Such miracles were represented as having been necessary in their time as means of attesting the revelation, which indeed did not publish doctrines contrary to reason but such as are above reason—which doctrines we have to hold as true on the basis of their supernatural attestation. Here, then, the dogmas are supported on miracles, but the miracles again upon the supra-rational dogma of the divine omnipotence, and on the proof of its historical reality to be adduced by reason. It is evident that this compromise is an untenable half-position, which can neither satisfy faith nor knowledge. It cannot satisfy faith; for faith wishes to find the divine presence and activity, not merely in rare individual events but everywhere in internal and external experience. Nor can it satisfy knowledge; for reason, when it has once become conscious of its right to the cognition of truth, will nowhere let a boundary-line be drawn where it has to cease to examine and begin blindly to believe. Reason can only co-ordinate the absolutely supra-rational and inconceivable with the anti-rational, which it must deny unless it would surrender itself; and in particular it cannot admit that nature is generally a regular order of events, while yet this order is broken in individual cases, and the connection of what exists in space and time is dissolved by events such that the conditions holding in the whole of the world of space and time were not present in them. It is, therefore, easily conceivable that supra-naturalism, with its halfness and unclearness, could not keep the enlightened rationalism from drawing its last consequences, and thinking the divine away out of the world without exception, so that the utterly empty abstraction of the "Supreme Being" alone remained—a Being beyond or outside of the world, and without active revelation in it, and consequently without religious significance. For how could there be possible a religious relation, a feeling of one's self as dependent and also as exalted, in reference to a Being of whom nothing further is known than that He is what is beyond the world—a negative bounding conception without any positive cognisable content, an unmoving secluded Being whose activity would be annulled by finite causes and put to rest, which therefore would enter into no real relation to us, and of which we would never experience any efficiency at all? An enlightenment which in this way makes God an empty Being, an unknowable essence, cuts through the vital nerve of religion. It has indeed been said that if the objects of faith can no longer be held to be proper realities, they still retain their high value as ideal images of the creative fantasy, through the æsthetic enjoyment of which the soul is raised above the common reality of things, and is calmed and edified. But it is difficult to take such consolation as meant in earnest; for although the pious man knows well that the highest truth which forms the content of his faith can only be known and expressed by him in figurative form, yet all the value and all the edifying power of these forms rest for him just on the fact that they are forms of a *true content*, that they are not mere inventions or fictions of our human imagination, but are the expression of a *reality* which is not only as true as, but even truer than, that of the world, because it makes all our knowing of the world possible and authenticates its truth. Take away from the pious man this conviction of the truth contained in the figurative language of religion, the conviction of the objective reality of the objects of his faith, and let these ideal images lose for him all earnest significance, how would he then be able any longer to worship that which he has now recognised as a form of his own creation? Such a strange substitute no one would ever have ventured even to offer as a compensation for the devastation of the faith effected by the *Aufklärung*, had it been considered—which many appear to have forgotten to-day — that the Alpha and Omega of all religion is reverence, that reverence is only possible for what is above us, and that nothing can be *above* us which is only *of* us, or is only the self-produced form of our subjective thoughts, wishes, and dreams.

Now, if all such compromises and pretended substitutes are insufficient, what then does there remain to religion in order to prevent the overthrow of its sanctuaries by the knowledge of the understanding? We do not require still to seek for the answer to this question. History itself has long since given it. The same weapon which inflicted the wound has also begun again to heal it. The thinking which sought to conquer the world and subject it to its conceptions in this process, lost God and its own self. But when it became aware of the fact that it profits a man nothing though he should gain the whole world and lose his own soul, it then began to go into itself and to reflect about itself. And, behold, it has found again in its own inner self the God which it was no longer able to find in the outer world! At the end of the last century there was repeated the same turn of thought which we find taking place in Greece four centuries before Christ. The superficial thinking of the *Aufklärung*, which clung to phenomena, was overcome by the deeper self-reflection of the Platonic philosophy, which found in the essence of the spirit the ground of being as well as of knowledge, the source and the rule of truth. This turn in the history of thought appeared decisively in modern times in the critical philosophy of Kant; but it was prepared by Berkeley's idealism and Hume's scepticism, by which the natural realism of the empiricists had been overcome. If science was again to find a positive relation to religion, it must first of all become clear regarding its own principle. That is, it must have recognised the one-sidedness of the two opposite principles of knowledge — namely, that of naïve natural realism or empiricism, and that of subjective idealism or rationalism—and it must have sought their synthesis in a deeper principle, in which the point of contact and connection with religion will at the same time be found.

Natural realism is the popular opinion that our knowledge of things is given to us simply through the perception of the senses. In this view the soul is represented as like an unwritten sheet of paper, or as a photographic plate, on which things make copies of themselves, so that they come into our consciousness exactly as they are in themselves. But Physics, Physiology, and Psychology have irrefutably shown how erroneous this popular realism is. Sounds do not lie in the vibrating bodies, or in the waves of air which proceed from them, but they arise first in our hearing ear; colours do not lie in vibrations of the ether, but arise only in our seeing eye; and the same holds true of the sensations of smell, taste, and touch. But even extension and motion depend for our consciousness on the perception of space, by which it is easy to perceive that they cannot be given to us from without. Just as little as the nerves of the eye, can those of the sense of touch convey into our consciousness spatial copies of bodies: on the contrary, the spatial image or perception can only be sketched by the self-activity of the soul—on the ground, it is true, of certain signs given in sensation. But if spatial extension and form are just as subjective as colour, sound, and smell, what remains of the material world of bodies? And what right have we then still to hold our perceptions to be simple copies of things themselves? Nay, more, what guarantee have we for holding that there are any things outside of us which correspond to them? What ground have we for determining whether our representations are not merely subjective? and whether our assumption of an existence of external things is not a pure prejudice sprung from the conceptions of substantiality and causality which have been arbitrarily fashioned by us? With this conclusion (which was drawn in Hume's scepticism) the world of the senses, which empirical realism had held to be the complete—or even the *only*—reality, became an unsubstantial appearance or phantasm, a chaos of impressions and representations of our consciousness, to which we are not entitled to ascribe either reality, or substantiality, or causality, or regulated order according to law, and which therefore hardly signify more than do the illusions of a confused dream. This was the natural and inevitable end of the empirical realism which made the knowing mind the passive receiver of a truth given from without.

It was Kant's merit that he carried back the truth of cognition to the laws and forms of our thinking and perceiving, which lie originally in the essence of the cognitive mind, and which are therefore universally valid. But, as it usually happens that a new principle carries its just opposition to the old principle to the excess of the opposite one-sidedness, so it happened also in the case of Kant. He started from the alternative that our conceptions either could arrange themselves according to the objects, or the objects according to our conceptions; and since the first view, that our conceptions depend on the objects, was the opinion of the empiricism which had dissolved itself in scepticism, Kant believed that, for his part, he could only put himself on the opposite side; and he set up the paradoxical proposition that our understanding is the lawgiver of nature—that is to say, in so far as nature consists only of our representations. Only to this do our forms of *thought*, according to Kant, extend; but they do not hold good of things *in themselves*, as these are independent of our consciousness. Taken exactly, Kant had no right even to accept the existence of things out of our consciousness, seeing that this view rests upon an inference of causality, while causality should not be accepted as valid when carried beyond the representations of our consciousness to trans-subjective things. With this position the Kantian philosophy fell into subjective idealism—which it does not indeed logically maintain, but which had already arisen as a consequence, derived from Kant's premises by his scholar Fichte.

But *subjective idealism* is just as untenable a principle of knowledge as empirical realism. If I can know nothing of any being beyond my consciousness, then the reality of the external world, inclusive of other men, is for me not merely a doubtful but even a worthless hypothesis, seeing that I should not stand in any relation with that which exists outside of me. Little as any one will carry out "Solipsism" in practical earnest, yet it is just as certainly the theoretical consequence of subjective idealism, which is thereby already reduced *ad absurdum*. But subjective idealism, moreover, does not even suffice for the explanation of our inner world of consciousness, for it leaves unexplained whence the sensations come to me which I find as given facts; and further, what distinguishes the real phenomena of my waking consciousness from images of my fantasy, from dreams and hallucinations? It leaves unexplained why I cannot proceed arbitrarily in combining my sensations into forms of perception in space and time, and in the arrangement of my representations according to logical categories. But I feel myself bound to a norm or rule, in the violation of which I fall into error. On the ground of subjective idealism there could properly be no error at all; for, if the matter of the sensations somehow given is indifferent to the forms of its connection brought to it by the autonomous understanding, there is no norm for the application of the various logical categories, and then there is also no abnormal or erroneous application of them that is contrary to truth. Nor can this difficulty be removed by appealing to the correspondence of the judgments of one individual with those of others; for, as subjective idealism denies the trans-subjective relation and validity of thinking, every Ego accordingly is hermetically shut up in the inner world of his sole consciousness: the world of consciousness of the one has no relations at all with the world of consciousness of others—which, moreover, is but a problematic world; it has no points of contact, no common means of finding its place in such a world: it therefore cannot possibly regulate itself according to these; nor, therefore, can it have in agreement with them the norm and control of its own correctness or truth. The uselessness of subjective idealism as a principle of knowledge shows itself most manifestly by this, that, in doing away with every norm for the recognition of truth, it also makes truth itself impossible. For there can only be truth and error in the judgment of the subjects where these know themselves to be bound to a common objective norm, to a principle of logical order which makes itself felt within every thinking subject as a binding law of its thinking, and which at the same time rises above the distinctions of all thinking subjects. Only the universal or divine reason, which, as the ground of all thinking and being, is the truth in itself, can also be the norm of our knowledge of truth.

We have thus again reached a result with regard to our true knowing similar to that which was reached in the last lecture with regard to our true willing according to duty. As the ground of moral obligation was not to be found either in the subject or in society, but only in the universal or divine will that combines both, so in like manner the ground of science, or of cognition generally, is neither to be found in the subject nor in the object *per se*, but only in the divine thinking that combines the two, which, as the common ground of the forms of thinking in all thinking minds, and of the forms of being in all beings, makes possible the correspondence or agreement between the former and the latter, or in a word, makes knowledge of truth possible. As morality is not in fact dependent in such a way on religion that certain particular duties are prescribed to it by a religious authority, yet certainly in this sense that it finds the ideal principle of all genuine moral willing and doing in its being bound to the absolute will of the good, or of God, so in like manner science is not bound in any individual act of knowledge to religious authority, but it can only really find the ground of the possibility of all true cognition in the fact of its being bound to the creative reason which is absolutely the truth. In this thought philosophical speculation was from the outset at one with religious mysticism. "In Thy light do we see light," says the Psalmist. According to St John, it is the Divine Logos who enlightens every man; and, according to St Paul, the Divine Spirit enables man even to know the deep things of God, and to judge everything independently. It is also a good Biblical thought that our knowing of the truth stands in essentially the same relation as our willing of the good. The knowing and the acting mind are not at all, as is now so often heard, two different kinds of minds, but are only two forms of the activity of one and the same mind, and they therefore also stand under essentially the same laws. Neither as knowing nor as willing can our mind correctly exercise itself if it put itself apart by itself and shut itself against the non-ego, the object, or society, or try to raise itself above them; for then it will either remain void of content, an empty form, or it will seek its content in arbitrary untrue ideas and in arbitrary ungood ends. Fantasticalness and libertinism have been often the offspring of subjective idealism. But, on the other hand, our mind can neither in its knowing nor in its willing receive its content simply from the external world; it would thereby cease to be a real mind, a self-activity, and it would become the thoughtless receptacle of extraneous dogmas that were not understood, and the unfree instrument of an alien will. Our mind can only rightly realise its essence in its thinking and willing if it stands in orderly reciprocal action with the world of things and men, if it subordinates itself in activity and passivity, in giving and taking, as a serving member to the organic order of the universe in which the divine spirit reveals itself as one, and yet in the variety of many gifts and powers.

Hence there result, regarding the relationship of religion and science, similar consequences as in the case of the relationship of religion and morality. With all the difference in their immediate objects, religion and science still hang so closely together in their ground and aim that their normal relationship will not be hostile opposition, but friendly mutual completion, while conflicts will only arise from abnormal tendencies and malformations of one or the other or both.

It may appear paradoxical to say that faith lies at the basis of all science, yet this cannot be disputed. All our knowing is formed from sensations and acts of thought which are carried on within our soul, and yet we believe that we know by these subjective functions the objective world, the reality which exists outside of us. This universal conviction is a *belief* which rests, not upon logical proofs, but upon the trust that our nature is so constituted that, when we correctly apply our powers of knowledge, we are not mocked by empty delusions, but are able to represent the reality of things in thoughts. But this involves the assumption that the real is also constituted for being thought by us, or that it is thinkable. But the real can only be thinkable if it is realised thought, a thought previously thought, which our thinking has only to think again. Therefore the real, in order to be thinkable for us, must be the realised thought of the creative thinking of an eternal divine reason, which is presented to our cognitive thinking. The confidence, therefore, that we, in our endeavour to know, do not merely move in subjective illusions and dreams, but that we copy the reality in our thinking, implicitly includes the confidence that the reality is the manifestation of the creative thoughts of the divine reason. Moreover, let us not forget that the assumption of the uniformity and immutable conformity to law of nature lies at the basis of all scientific induction—an assumption which is manifestly not to be proved, and which therefore can only be accepted by faith. This, however, includes in itself the further assumption that the whole of nature is ruled by a single principle—and, indeed, since laws are ideal relations, by a single spiritual principle, an ordering reason. Hence, rightly viewed, it is religious belief which is presupposed by all scientific knowledge as the basis of its possibility. Naturally, this presupposition need not be present as conscious conviction in the case of every one who cultivates science: just as little as in the case of every one who acts morally from a feeling of duty must there be present the consciousness of his being bound by the universal divine will. But it must always still remain true that both in the feeling of duty, and also in reliance on the truth of our thinking, religious belief in the divine ground of our selves, and of the world, is to be posited implicitly as an accompanying presupposition. To raise this *unconscious* assumption into consciousness is the task of the philosopher who analyses the process of knowledge—that is to say, in so far as he actually goes down to the foundation of things, and does not, as mostly happens in the present day, stop short where the decisive questions just begin.

As science rests upon a belief, the actual, although unconscious, belief in a world-ordering divine reason, it also finds its final goal only in the thought of God. Its proximate goal certainly is everywhere the connection and ordering of the manifold facts given by experience, the finding out of the connection between phenomena and of the laws which govern the different groups of phenomena. In doing so, as long as it merely investigates the connections of individual things in a limited sphere, it of course need not have recourse to God, who is certainly not an individual substance or an individual cause alongside of others; and therefore we perfectly understand how an astronomer like Laplace confessed that he did not need the hypothesis of a God for the explanation of the mechanism of the heavenly bodies. Yet the particular groups of phenomena with which the individual sciences have to do, nevertheless do not stand isolated with reference to each other, but they are all connected with each other. Hence, the knowledge obtained in none of them can come to a final satisfying conclusion; it always points beyond this narrow circle to a wider connection, to higher laws, and to more general principles. Now it is the task of the universal science, philosophy, to connect the principles of the individual sciences with each other, and, by carrying them back to *one* universal supreme principle, to seek the ultimate conclusion of knowledge generally. In continuation of this same procedure, according to which we seek everywhere unknown causes for given facts, philosophy as the universal science seeks in a supreme principle the hypothetical ground for the explanation of the universe or of the world as such. The often-heard assertion that it thereby oversteps its bounds is a prejudice for which no real grounds can be adduced, and which is rather explained as arising only from a temporary sceptical discouragement and weariness of scientific thinking. Sigwart says admirably at the close of his 'Logic':—

"The metaphysical close of the explanation of the world forms the presupposition without which no desire to know in the proper and strict sense is at all possible; it goes beyond the facts given in experience in no other direction than every attempt to conceive what is given as fact does so. With the same right with which we build up in the individual substances and their powers an intelligible kingdom as the ground of phenomena, and pressed by the same impulse to embrace in a unity what is dispersed, we also take a further step towards an ultimate explanation of the world, according to the demands or obligations of our thinking. What separates metaphysics from the rest of science is not its method, for method in regard to all knowing is at the last absolutely the same; it is only the universality of its task, and this task itself is as necessary as that of knowing generally. It stands at the beginning of all science, seeing that it brings into clearness the principles which all scientific striving presupposes; it stands at the end of all science, seeing that its presuppositions can only authenticate themselves by the result—viz., the thorough-going agreement of all knowledge. Metaphysics will therefore remain a work of partial knowledge, as all knowing is knowing in part so long as the finite thinking has not expanded and raised itself into the divine."

Thus far it has also been already indicated that science, in its attempt to find a final philosophical explanation of the existing world, never will nor can reach a completely satisfying definitive result. We can only predicate of the unconditioned principle of the world such positive determinations as we have derived from the world of our experience, be it natural, or spiritual, or both. But these predications which spring from the world of the manifold and conditioned can of course only inadequately designate the essence of the one unconditioned being; they can only pass as analogical and symbolical determinations which would express that we think of the essence of the basis of the world as being in a certain, yet always only relative, similarity with such or such phenomena of our inner or outer experience. It is conceivable that science, when oppressed by this difficulty in the determination of the absolute principle of the world, should often, on the one hand, renounce the attempt to reach a single explanation of the world, and, on the other, believe that it must be contented with the most indefinite and lowest determinations of the principle of the world, such as being, force, matter, motion, and suchlike. In the former case it comes to no determination of knowledge at all, to no answer to the questions as to the Whence and Whither of existence which are always moving men; and thereby all particular knowing becomes uncertain and doubtful, the courage of the inquirer is paralysed by doubt, and the energy of the impulse of knowledge is tied down. In the other case the result is untrue explanations of the world, arising from insufficient principles, such as materialism and positivism. With this result the higher spheres of life are just those which remain inexplicable; and, in order to get rid of the inexplicable, the proper character and significance of the spiritual, moral, and religious life is ignored, and everything is reduced to the level of the lowest physical phenomena; and the actual world is therefore not explained, but mutilated and distorted. Materialistic aberrations and sceptical distraction, indifference, want of intelligence for the great connections and universal ideas, with a pedantic squandering and losing of one's self in the most minute and puny matters—these are the dangers which, as experience shows, threaten science in times of philosophical disheartenment. In presence of such dangers it is religion which, by its idea of God as sprung from the inner experiences of the soul and corresponding to them, always sharpens the conscience anew, and rouses it to strive unweariedly in the prosecution of its *highest* task — namely, to seek for a principle for the explanation of the world which will be truly and universally satisfying. Not that science should therefore at once accept the religious idea of God upon authority, and employ it for its explanation of the world. In so doing it would but too easily overlook its proper task of rising step by step from the particular and gradually approaching the ultimate principles of things, and it would lose the capacity of proving all things, even the religious ideals, and holding fast only the best of all. But science will certainly behold in the religious idea of God the symbolical anticipation of the goal to which it has itself not to soar upon the wings of fantasy, but to climb along the toilsome and endless way of the thinking understanding. It will always be compelled to say to itself that the religious spirit, which draws *its* highest principle, not from the wide breadth of universal experience, but out of the depths of the inner moral-religious experience, does not merely as such belong to the whole of the reality which is to be explained, but that it occupies in this whole the very highest position and significance, so that consequently every explanation of the world is insufficient and erroneous which leaves no place for these highest facts of experience, and which stands in contradiction to the necessary demands of the moral-religious spirit. Religion, therefore, without wishing to impede the work of science in detail, or to keep it under its tutelage, will yet be regulative with regard to science in so far as it sets before science in symbolical form the goal which it must keep in view and strive after in order to fulfil, at least approximately, its task of an ultimate explanation of the world.

That which is a task for science, an ideal that it has always to strive after and yet will never completely attain—namely, the highest Idea of Truth that completes and concludes all knowledge—is possessed by religion. Religion, however, does not possess it in the form of conceptual knowledge that satisfies the scien-

tific thinking, but in the form corresponding to the
presentient soul, of the symbol or of the significant
sign. Hence religion needs for the correct interpretation of its signs the completing and correcting help
of science, just as much as science needs religion.
So long as the forms in which the religious spirit
objectifies its inner experiences to itself are yet
transparent enough to let their inner real sense be
recognised, and so long as they still remain in harmony with the universal view of the world, so long
will they not be felt as an impediment, but will serve
religious elevation as its natural means. But when
the creative power of the religious spirit dries up, its
forms and faith are then wont to become petrified, and
what was at the beginning a transparent veil of truth
becomes then a hard covering behind which the spiritual
content is so concealed that it is hardly longer recog-
nisable by any one. What at the beginning was only
a means, then becomes an end in itself; what at the
beginning was the expression of a really present common belief, then becomes a compulsory yoke, which
produces a mere external uniformity of confession by
the subjection of men's minds to a formula that is not
understood. And if at the same time the general consciousness of the world in the course of the advance
of civilisation experiences such profound transformations as has been the case with the Christian peoples
since the awakening of the sciences of nature and

history, then the contradiction between the old believed notions that rest upon quite other assumptions and the present knowledge becomes more and more glaring, and doubt of the truth of the traditional dogmas always rises up more earnestly, and with it doubt of the truth of the religion which men had been accustomed to identify with those dogmas. In this state of matters some put themselves on the side of the secular knowledge or even of the latest and boldest hypotheses which are given out as science, and they triumphantly proclaim the near end of religion, having no presentiment that religion, as well as science and art, morals and law, is a constitutive element of human nature, and therefore may pass through the most manifold developments, but can never cease as long as there are men. On the other hand, others put themselves on the side of religion, defend all its traditional doctrines and dogmas as ostensibly infallible divine revelations, and combat with all the weapons at their command the results of science as a vain delusion invented and diffused by bad men. Thus the antagonism between faith and knowledge has become so acute at the present day, that many despair of any possibility of a reconciliation and mediation of them.

According to what has been now said, we do not see ourselves compelled to share this pessimistic view of the situation. Rather are we of opinion that a little calm self-reflection would only be needed on both sides to recognise that both parties stand in their ultimate aims much nearer than is supposed, and that there is much more reason for them to learn mutually from each other than to exhaust their powers in a blind conflict. Science, as we saw, will have to remember that its acceptance of the knowableness of the world, if it is not to be without a principle at all, can only be supported on a belief in the creative divine reason in which the agreement of the forms of thinking and being is grounded, and in which consequently the truth of our thinking is guaranteed. It will have to recall the fact that the world of nature or of external sensible phenomena, the investigation of which it pursues with so much zeal and success, is nevertheless only the one side of reality, along with which consists the inner side of our own psychological life as the much more important half of reality; and therefore that an explanation of the world which would ignore this more important side, and which would take the principle of the universe only from the external world of phenomena, would commit the most prodigious abstraction, and, in spite of all fortunate discoveries in detail, would yet at bottom miss the truth on the whole. On the other side, the representatives of religion will also have to remember that they possess the treasure of spiritual truth always only in earthen vessels—that is, in symbolical representations—on which their earthly and temporal origin is but too clearly impressed for them to be able to put forth a permanent claim to infallible divine truth; and consequently that the striving of the thinking mind to distinguish between the eternal truth and its temporal vesture, between the spiritual kernel and its sensible shell, is not an act of sacrilege, but a service which is performed for the sacred cause of truth, and therefore of God. It is not to be doubted that this service of truth is not accomplished without pain and sacrifice, when so many ideas that have become dear prove themselves to be but perishable earthly vessels; but these pains are the price to be paid for obtaining the most precious of treasures—namely, a conviction which establishes the heart. Piety will lose nothing of its humility and trust if it perceives the governing of divine omnipotence no longer in rare supernatural incidents but in the whole constant order of nature, and if single spots of history are no longer to be separated out as the sanctuaries of a unique mysterious revelation, but the whole development of the moral and religious life of humanity becomes the revelation of educating wisdom and love. If science helps religion to attain to this deepening of its insight and widening of its view, ought it not then to be rather treasured as a friend of religion instead of being feared as its foe? At the present time, indeed, the two still stand in a state of violent feud; but the time will come when they will mutually understand each other better, and will be united in the harmonious worship of God in spirit and in truth.

LECTURE IV.

THE BELIEF IN GOD: ITS ORIGIN AND DEVELOPMENT.

KANT has said that there are especially two things which excite our reverence: the starry heaven above us, and the moral law within us. He has thus indicated the two sources from which the belief in God springs—namely, the external world in so far as it shows to our thinking a rational order of existing being, an all-embracing truth; and the internal world in so far as in it a rational order of being that-ought-to-be presses itself upon us as an all-determining end, or the ideal of the good. That the good which we oppose to actuality as that which ought to be, is yet not merely our subjective thought, a dream of our imagination, but that it is that which truly *is*, the power that is over reality; and that the principle of the whole external existence is not alien and indifferent to the ideal longing and hoping of our own being, but is the source of its motive power and the guarantee of its right to realisation,—this is the kernel of the belief in God. The idea of God is the Unity of the True and the Good, or of the two highest ideas which our reason thinks as theoretical reason and demands as practical reason; and if reason is not to lose its unity, and therefore itself, in this antagonism between knowing of the real and demanding of the ideal, it must raise itself above the opposition to the synthesis of the two sides, or to the idea of God. This is the *a priori* ground or rational origin of the belief in God found in the nature of our mind.

It is of course evident of itself that this principle, as we have here expressed it, was not from the very beginning in the consciousness of men; for, in order to think ideas, reason must already be developed, which in the first of mankind it could just as little be as in children. This, however, does not exclude the fact that there was from the beginning the unconscious rational impulse which lay at the basis of the formation of the belief in God, however manifold may have been the direct motives which co-operated with it. All traces of the oldest history of religion point to this, that the belief in God did not exist ready-made from the beginning, but that it was formed out of the prehistorical belief in spirits contemporaneously with the beginnings of social civilisation, on the threshold of the historical life of the peoples. And the original belief in spirits appears already to point back to two sources—to external nature and the soul of man. For *ancestral spirits* and *nature-spirits* are found everywhere in the primeval period of the peoples side by side with one another, and passing into each other in various forms of combination without the one being able to be referred to the other. They appear to be both equally original, and to be explained by different psychological motives.

Various naïve reflections may have contributed to the universally diffused belief of the primitive men in the continued existence and active presence of the souls of the dead. When they saw life disappear in the dying with the fleeting breath, it was natural to find the principle of life, or the soul, in the breath; and hence in most languages the words for Soul and Spirit coincide with the designations for Breath and Wind. But that the soul that flees with the breath does not perish, but only changes its place of residence, was testified to primitive man by his dream-perceptions, in which he saw the dead again appear. From this he concluded that they continued to live as aeriform shadowy beings, usually invisible, and that they moved more rapidly than when they lived in the body, penetrated everywhere, and were superior in knowledge and capability to earthly men. The incorporeal double of the dead person could, according to the primitive belief, assume the most different and most frightful forms; it could work at a distance, transport itself with the swiftness of lightning to other places, and could otherwise produce wonderful effects beyond the measure of what is natural to mankind. Besides, the spirits of ancestors remained, according to the oldest view, in the neighbourhood of the families they had left behind, and in constant relation with them; they claimed a share of the daily meals and other marks of honour; they rewarded such performances by the protection of their kin; and they punished the neglect of these things by sensible evils.

But the spirit-host believed in by primitive men was recruited not merely from the world of men, but also from that of nature. The intermediate link between the human souls and those with which the untutored fancy peopled nature may have been formed by the souls of animals, the worship of which played a great part in Egypt, and which are even now objects of worship among savage tribes. In everything which moves on earth or in the heavens, and which consequently appears to live, the primitive man beheld an active soul as the subject and cause of the respective movements. Fountains, rivers and seas, trees and woods, winds and waves, and in particular also the earthly fire of the hearth and the heavenly fire of the storm, and finally the sun, moon, and stars, and the heaven that embraces all,—all these appeared to the naïve fantasy as living beings, because its "personifying apperception" was able to apprehend the subject of phenomena only as an active subject after the analogy of the human soul. This animation of nature is not to be explained by holding that the primitive man only compared natural phenomena with living beings, or even that he merely thought of them as a domicile or operation of spirits of human origin. Either view would presuppose a definite distinguishing of the sensible element and of the supersensible subject; but such a distinction only appeared later, whereas, for the original mythological notion, the sensible element and the subject that was active in it still coincided as one. It is only on this view that all those names, attributes, and myths of the natural Deities are explained, which manifestly have their roots in natural phenomena. I can therefore not agree with those who, after the example of the ancient rationalist Euhemeros, would explain the natural Deities from elevation of ancestral spirits to be rulers over earthly and heavenly regions—a view which is advocated, for instance, by Mr Herbert Spencer. I believe that they explain themselves more simply, without going round about by human souls, from the animation of nature, which was just as natural for the childlike fantasy of the primitive man as it still is to-day for children and poets. Only so much may perhaps be admitted, that for the more definite personifications of the nature-spirits, for their separation from the element of nature, and their elevation to be the objects of a standing and common cult, the undoubtedly more original cult of ancestral spirits may have co-operated.

Nevertheless this prehistoric belief in spirits cannot yet be properly called religion; it only contained the germs of religion. The development of these germs, however, could not be reached before the beginnings of social organisation and order. So long as men still lived in roaming hordes without social organisation, there was also still merely an indefinite swarm of spirits without individual qualities, only perhaps that the friendly spirits were distinguished from the hostile (light spirits from dark spirits). It was not till families gathered around the domestic altar (the hearth) as settled households, till these families expanded into clans, and till the clans united into tribes, that there also arose out of the swarm of common spirits the Gods proper as the protecting powers of the corresponding groups of human society. And with these groups there also grew at the same time their ideal representatives, the divine patron spirits or tutelary genii. The families had only their narrowly limited house-gods; the religion of the clans and tribes rose to the worship of higher common tutelary Deities,— whether it was that the ancestral spirit of a prominent family, of a chief, or of the founder of a city, rose to the rank of a common God of the people, or that the local cult of a nature-spirit became the connecting centre for a greater group of the surrounding dwellers, and thereby the (elementary) tutelary spirit of the place was transformed into the tutelary spirit of the community of the region and into the founder of their state, and was identified with a tribal hero or put into genealogical connection with one. Thus there arose out of the deification of ancestral spirits and the humanisation of nature-spirits, the world of the Gods of the several national religions. In the case of many of these mythical forms it will always remain obscure how they fashioned themselves in the consciousness of their votaries,—whether by a nature-spirit, to which a certain place was sacred, becoming the tutelary God of the settlers on his territory, and thus becoming their *Heros eponymus*, or by a historical ancestor with the growing power of his clan being raised to be the ruler also of their natural surroundings, of the land, sea, and sky. So much appears at all events to be certain (as it is put in the words of Goblet d'Alviella), "that in the classical mythology there is found a continual interaction between the Gods and heroes: if Gods are represented as glorified men, it is no wonder that glorified men also come to be regarded as Gods."

With the elevation of the tutelary spirits of definite social human groups above the other spirits, the beginning of the religious belief in Gods was made. An organised Polytheism, however, was not yet reached everywhere, but this only came about in those peoples who attained to a certain degree of culture and a lasting political unity. Ideas of a divine hierarchy developed themselves everywhere *pari passu* with the improvement of the earthly political institution. And men were also quite conscious of this parallelism between the heavenly and earthly kingdom, but by a natural perspective deception they always held the human community to be a copy of the heavenly. But what distinguishes these Gods of the Polytheistic national religions from the spirits, is not merely the greater power and dominion attributed to them, but also a new and higher content and purpose of their life: they are the bearers, founders, and preservers of the world-order—not only of the natural, but also of the moral, order of the world. The spirits worshipped by savage tribes are individual powers which act by caprice and chance, which combat with each other, perish, and are supplanted by new spirits. The savages are never sure that the sun which sets to-day will appear again to-morrow, or that the summer which is now overcome by the giant winter will return again next year. As their own life is still driven on without content and purpose by momentary impulses, so also is it with the life of their swarms of spirits. The higher belief, and properly the first religious belief in Gods, has been gained from two sides—from the formation of a social order among men, and from intellectual reflection upon the order of things in the life of nature, which both co-operated to bring about the same result.

Because the beginnings of all social orders and practices, from the government of the house up to the government of the State, had been essentially formed under the influence of religious motives, it was inevitable that the Gods should be thought of as the founders and protectors of these orders and practices: not that they had from the very beginning also represented moral ideals of a universal kind—for such were not yet known to primitive men, nor could they therefore ascribe them to their Gods—but they were certainly the representatives of the abiding collective will and the common wellbeing of the community of their worshippers. Accordingly, every violation of this whole or of its individual members, by which the existence and wellbeing of the family, the tribe, and the people is violated, is at the same time a trespass against the divine power that protects this community. Hence in the primitive States the administration of justice stood everywhere in closest connection with religion. The social obligations were strengthened by the oath, the appeal to divine witnesses and avengers; and the Gods aided the discovery of criminals by oracles or divine judgments, which played everywhere an important part in times of crude administration of law. The expiation of a crime by punishment or voluntary restitution is everywhere at the same time a religious expiation for the reconciliation of the offended Deity. Now the more this rational side of the divine government, directed to the good of the moral order of the human community, gained in significance for practical piety and took precedence over its physical working, so much the more was it also necessary for the representation of the personal character of the Gods to be put into harmony with their social governing for the common advantage. Men began to represent the protecting powers of society as types of the qualities valued in society, and consequently to represent them as *moral ideals;* not of course in the sense which *we* are wont to connect with a moral ideal, but in the sense that the existing ideas of human ability held by the peoples were personified in the Gods themselves. In particular, the artistic fantasy of the Greeks succeeded in developing their Gods into ideals of that καλοκἀγαθία, of that beautiful morality of symmetry, of the harmonious balance of reason and morality, in which they beheld the ideal of human virtue. It is certainly not to be thought that this higher representation of the moral being of the Deity was anywhere the universal popular view; it was, in fact, everywhere originally only present in the knowledge of individual enlightened men, and had to assert itself laboriously in constant conflict against the cruder ideas of the mass of the people. It is well known how keenly the Greek philosophers, from Heraclitus and Xenophanes, protested against the immoral representations of the national religion. And around what else did the struggle of the Hebrew prophets against the obtuseness of the crowd turn than just the opposition between the moral conception of the Deity and the naturalistic mythological conception? Perhaps we may see in this opposition the proper turning-point of the history of religion, even more than in the question about the unity or plurality of the divine, which indeed is connected with it, although the two do not quite coincide.

In two respects the awaking reflection on the order of nature has been of great importance for the development of the belief in God, side by side with the progress of the social order. When men began to reflect upon the regularity in the succession of the times of the day and year, and their connection with the motion of the heavenly bodies, the thought could not but press itself upon them that the powers which rule in nature do not act according to arbitrariness and caprice, but that they stand, just like men, under a constant and common order. This order they could then refer either to the prescription of a supreme God standing above nature, or to the reign of law indwelling in the universe itself, which, as a universal power above the individual Gods, was partly personified in particular genii, and partly expressed in abstract conceptions. The Egyptian Maat, daughter of the sun-god Ra, and the Persian genius Asha Vahista were personifications of the natural and moral order of the world; and for the same thought the Hindus had the impersonal conceptions Rita and Karma, the Greeks had Μοῖρα and Νέμεσις, and the Chinese had Tao. In so far as by all these expressions there was designated a world-ruling power superior to the many individual Gods, there is clearly betrayed the consciousness that the many Gods are not yet the highest, that the really divine still lies above them; and this therefore shows a Monotheistic tendency. The transition to Monotheism has, however, been made in two different ways, which led to different conceptions of the Monotheistic thought of God. The one of these ways which was taken by the Hindus and the Greeks proceeds from the phenomena of nature, and leads through continued abstraction and generalisation to a single substance and universal law, or to Pantheism; the other way proceeds from the limited national God, and leads through the expansion of his sphere of power and the moralisation of his nature to ethical *Theism*, the classical representatives of which have been the prophets of Israel.

It is quite conceivable that a people disposed for philosophical reflection, like the Hindus and Greeks, may have come early to the thought that the many

Nature-Gods were only different forms of the manifestation of one and the same divine Being; but it is also conceivable that the propensity to abstraction and generalisation, when once awakened, could not come to rest before it had resolved the manifold manifestations into the unity of a universal Being which, because all distinctions have been obliterated in it, is only an empty indeterminate abstract Being which is hardly distinguished from nothing. Certainly it was a step in the progress of the religious spirit that the Deity was no longer thought of as a finite object along with other objects, but that the thought of infinitude, of opposition to all limited worldly existence, was taken up in earnest. - But the infinite was still conceived of in a one-sidedly negative way, in the Brahmanic and Eleatic speculation, as the abyss which swallows up all finite being, not as the positive ground which produces and maintains the finite. The Brahma of the Vedanta philosophy, like the *one* infinite Being of Parmenides, is like the cave of the lion, into which all the footsteps lead, but none lead out again. If the true is only the most abstract distinctionless and changeless Being, then the world of manifold and changeable existence is an untrue appearance, a delusion of Maya, which indeed becomes the more inconceivable, seeing that the subject and its consciousness—for which the appearance of the manifold and changeable exists—has itself also but an apparent existence like everything else. Thus does the Pantheism of the absolute substance show itself as Akosmism, and ultimately as absolute Illusionism. As in this infinite there disappear with all other distinctions also the distinctions of true and false, of weal and woe, of good and bad, the religious disposition can here only consist in indolent brooding over the nothingness of existence, in indifference to all the interests of life, and finally in the extinguishing of the living will itself—"Nirvana."

While the Indian mind had lost itself in the mazes of Pantheism, Akosmism, and Illusionism, the more energetic thinking of the Greeks was happily able to overcome this stage of transition, and to rise to a view of God and the world which was destined to be of the greatest importance for the religious development of humanity. Plato, like the Eleatic philosophy, had also distinguished between the world of sense, which is only apparent reality, and the "really real," which is elevated above space and time. But this really real being, according to Plato, is not, as with the Eleatics, an abstract unity that excludes all distinctions, and consequently also all thinking, but it is a world of thoughts, the plurality of which is unified by inner necessity into a harmonious whole; and thus it forms the world of the true, the beautiful, and the good. This world of ideas is embraced into a unity in the highest Idea, the Idea of God, which at the same time is perfect being. In God (the divine reason) there lies not only the ultimate ground of all knowing and being, or of all truth, but also the ultimate end of all being, or the good. That God's essential being is the good, that all statements regarding God are to be measured by the idea of the good, and that He is therefore as much the ground of justice in the moral world as of truth and beauty in the natural world,—these are central thoughts of the Platonic philosophy, the high historical significance and abiding truth of which stand fast, although it may also have to be recognised that its original intuitions were still affected with the limits of the Greek thinking. It was a lofty idealism which saw in the world the revelation of a divine reason, a system of archetypal ideas, which the human spirit represents in its knowledge of truth. But this idealism had still as its reverse side the dualism between the Idea and the irrational reality, which is not the pure expression of the Idea, but stands in partial opposition to it. For, when the Ideas enter into manifestation they are drawn out of one another into the dividedness of space and time, and are thus as it were displaced and distorted. The sensible world is therefore only the imperfect obscured representation or copy of the pure world of true being, or of the Ideas. The cause of this imperfectness is the irrational principle of the "unbounded" or of exteriority and succession in time, a principle which is properly a non-existing being, $\mu\dot{\eta}\ \ddot{o}\nu$;

but as the contributory cause of the world of appearance it yet again becomes a negative quantity, a matter adverse to the Idea, which hinders the pure manifestation of the Idea. With this division of the ideal and sensible world a mediation of the two was needed, and this was found by Plato in the soul of the world and of man which stands in the middle between reason and sense. These thoughts, the opposition of the two worlds and their mediation through a middle principle, became of immense importance for the following time. But they have their root in Plato in this position, that the spirit, when it began to reflect upon itself, was at first conscious only of its distinction from the external world, but not yet of its autocratic power over it; and this, again, is connected with the fact that it apprehended its specific nature first in thinking, and not in moral willing, that it recognised as its task only the copying the given harmony of the world, and not the free shaping of the world and realising of its own ideal in the world. It is the Greek Intellectualism and Æstheticism, the want of ethical depth and power, which forms the limit of the Platonic idealism and the ground of that dualism which does not let the Divine Spirit come to full lordship over the real world. The same dualism may be also observed in the philosophy of Aristotle. He, indeed, finds everywhere in the world rational purposes (thoughts of final ends) as the working "Form" of things; but this rational principle has always to combat with the irrational principle of matter which is contrary to purpose and conception, and its resistance is never entirely to be overcome. According to Aristotle, God is pure Form without matter, pure activity without passivity and change; but such Form is only pure thinking, which again has only itself as its content. As this activity of thought which persists in itself (νόησις νοήσεως), God is separated from the world which is mixed up of activity and passivity; He is indeed the self-unmoved cause of the motion of the world, in so far as the imperfect strives after His perfectness, but He does not rule over it, and He does not come to revelation in it. As the philosophical thinker after Aristotle felt himself in the consciousness of his higher dignity exalted above the cares of the practical life, so, according to him, God is infinitely exalted in the stillness of His eternal unchangeable thinking above the world of becoming, of striving, and of struggling, in nature and humanity, which is a world full of change and suffering. This philosophical transcendence was combined by the Epicureans with the popular Polytheism in such a way that they thought of the regions intermediate between heaven and earth as inhabited by Gods, who lead by themselves a cheerful life of enjoyment without troubling themselves in any way about earthly things and the affairs of men. The Stoics, on the other hand, went back again to the world-soul of the Ionic philosophy of nature; they thought of the Deity partly as the primal material of the world, the fire out of which all proceeded and into which all again returns, and partly as the world-reason, the Logos which guides and orders all, the all-wise Providence. This latter side became so very predominant among the later Stoics that their conception of God, which at the beginning was more of a naturalistic Pantheistic character, always approached more to an immanent ethical Monotheism. But as the Stoics did not wish wholly to lose touch with the mythological faith of the people, they received into their system the national Gods as the subordinate forms of the manifestation of the one Deity, or as Its ministering organs. The same was also done by the Neo-Platonists, who needed these half-divine middle beings ("demons") the more urgently as they carried the Platonico-Aristotelian view of the Deity as belonging to a world beyond this to its utmost issue; they divested the Deity of all positive attributes, and made It a wholly incognisable Being which, inaccessible to clear thinking, can only be felt by ecstatic feeling. As the ancient philosophy thus ended with Agnosticism, it was indeed able to further the dissolution of the mythological Polytheism, but it could put nothing positive that could satisfy the religious feeling in place of the old. The substitute for the old belief in God could only be formed by the new faith which had developed itself out of the religion of Israel.

The belief of the Hebrews in their tribal God Jahve had in the pre-prophetic time hardly yet distinguished itself clearly from the analogous belief of the other Semitic tribes in their tribal Deities. The belief was first brought to a higher development by the prophets, who raised the tribal God of Israel to be the God of the world, by identifying Him with the moral good in the same way as Plato did some centuries later, and by thinking of His government as an exhibition of holy justice, which has only the good itself as its end, and which does not let itself be determined by any partial collateral considerations, not even by those which related to national privileges. To the Hebrew prophets Jehovah indeed always remained the God of Israel in a peculiar sense, but His government of the world had nevertheless a universal end, which passed beyond the national limits and was unconditionally valuable in itself; and this end it had to realise in the establishment of a kingdom of righteousness and peace in Israel, and from Israel outwards in mankind generally. The prophets, while believing in the victory of this moral end of the divine government of the world, also already looked with hope to the time when the God of this moral government would be the only God of all the peoples. Besides, it was favourable to the religion of Israel that a Polytheistic mythology, already deeply rooted in the fantasy of the people, did not stand here opposed to the higher moral idea of God, as was the case among the Indians and Greeks. Even the anthropomorphic traits, which were by no means wanting in the belief in Jahve, were however not of the same kind as in the more sensuous Polytheistic religions. No such myths were told of Jahve as of Zeus and Jupiter. If the popular belief ascribed passions to Jahve, such as wrath and jealousy, it was not difficult for the prophets to interpret these passions morally as the reaction of the holy God against the human sin and guilt which resisted His purpose of good. Such moral anger and punishment, however, does not exclude the faithfulness and long-suffering of God in carrying out His good purpose, but it serves the realisation of the moral ideal by means of the chastisement and purification of the sinful people. From this point of view the history of their people became to the prophets the advancing revelation of the educating wisdom and justice and grace of their God, who also holds the fortunes of nations in His hand and guides them to the final end of realising His all-embracing kingdom, in which righteousness, peace, and salvation will reign. Nor could the misfortunes in their experience disconcert the prophets in this faith in the moral teleology of the government of the world; for all the adversity of the present only turned their hopeful look further away and higher towards the much more glorious ideals of the future. In the consciousness of the prophets, God, just because He was one with the moral Ideal, became the God of the historical revelation, the Lord of the times and seasons, who in His decrees disposes of all that is in the future. The Hebrew did not, like the Greek, find the revelation of God in the harmony of an ideal world of thoughts which was always immanent in the actual, but he found that revelation in the purposive striving of the whole of history, in which all that is actual is continually transcended and directed by the ideal of the future.

In the spirit of the great prophets the two sides of the thought of God were combined in the closest way— namely, the exaltation of the holy One above human weakness and sin, and the condescension of the gracious One to a helpful presence. But in the post-exilian Judaism the first side of the Idea predominated so strongly, that God was then thought of almost only as a lawgiver and a judge in the other world, and men could only see His revelation in humanity mediated through middle beings like the angels and the personified Wisdom, or the personified Word. Judaism had therefore at last arrived at the same dualistic transcendence of the Deity as the Platonic idealism; and thus the same need showed itself on both sides to fill up the gulf between this world and the world beyond by intermediate beings. The religious philosophy of the Alexandrian Jew Philo was a product of these converging currents of the time. According to Philo, God is not merely not to be thought of in an anthropomorphic way as like men, but He is without attributes at all, and exalted above all conceptions and names; we can only know of Him *that* He is, not *what* He is; we can only call Him the existing One and the cause of all being. His working upon the world is not immediate, but is mediated through other powers which are embraced in the divine " Logos." This Logos is the image and the first-born Son of God, the ideal of the world, and the Mediator of its creation and government, and of all the revelation of God in sacred history. This shadowy form of the Philonic Logos, which wavers between conceptual abstraction and personality, could naturally not suffice to satisfy the religious need of a real historical revelation of God; but its great historical significance consisted in this, that it prepared the conceptual form for the theological apprehension and expression of the new revelation in Jesus Christ.

Jesus recognised in the God of the prophets and of the Psalms his heavenly Father and the heavenly Father of us all, who makes His sun rise on the just and the unjust, who condescends to the miserable and sinners in compassionate love in order to make them His children and associates of His kingdom, the imitators and instruments of His own holy love. The God-consciousness of Jesus was not indeed a Hellenic cheerful consciousness, as has been said; his God was rather the holy One of Israel infinitely exalted above the sinful beings of the world. The requirements of

His will were not lowered by Jesus, but were raised into a demand for the surrender of the whole man to the one unconditioned purpose of God; and the essence of the kingdom of God has been set forth by him in sharpest contrast to the kingdoms of this world and their glory, which must be renounced by whoever would win the kingdom of heaven. But while Jesus maintained the religious ideal in its unconditioned exaltedness and purified it, on the other hand he at the same time bridged over the gulf which had opened up to the whole ancient world, Jewish as well as Greek, between the ideal and the actual, the good and the true. To him the holy God was not merely the exacting lawgiver, the reckoning Lord, the retributive judge, but He was above all the loving Father, who sees in every man His child, the object of His merciful care and wise training, the God who does not even cast out and condemn the sinner, but who will and can save him, deliver him from his sin, and raise him to the good. The good is indeed the Ideal, the kingdom of God, which is not yet actually here, but has yet "to come" and be actual; yet this Ideal is already an internal efficient present power, the power of the Spirit of God, who drives demons out of souls; the power of faith and hoping trust, which removes mountains; and the power of love, which by serving and bearing overcomes the evil of the world and unites men into a harmonious family of God. In the religious idealism of Jesus, God is therefore not merely the perfect ideal of the good, but also the self-realising power of the good, on which every resistance of the world must ultimately break in pieces, and which therefore shows itself the superior power over reality as the true kernel of being. The synthesis of the good and true was for the first time realised in full depth and with clear consciousness in Jesus' Idea of God; and therefore it is rightly accepted by us as the highest revelation of God which still remains authoritative, however much the unfolding of it in conceptions and its mediation with secular truth may always remain the inexhaustible problem of the religious thinking of humanity.

With this revelation of God, which had become personal life in Jesus, the national limitedness and the legal externality of the Jewish belief in God were overcome. The God of the prophets could now become in the missionary preaching of Paul the world-reconciling God of the world of the nations; and in the mysticism of John it became the love which makes its dwelling in the hearts of the pious, and unites them into a fellowship of brethren and of true worshippers of God. It was natural that this new belief in God should seek after new forms of expression, and should express the fulness of its contents in the language of the philosophical thinking of that time. The Philonic conception of the Logos presented itself as the most natural means for accomplishing this. By its application to the revelation of God which had appeared in Jesus, the alliance between Jewish theology and Greek philosophy was concluded, and from it the doctrine of God of the Christian Church proceeded. The historical purposiveness of this doctrinal development cannot be contested even by those who by no means hold its doctrinal formulas as final truth. This development rests upon two grounds. On the one hand, by combination with the Logos of speculation the religious revelation of Jesus was divested of its accidental historical investments, such as lay in the national and apocalyptic idea of the Messiah, which the earliest Christians had shared with the Jews, as appears from their expectation of a visible second coming of Christ from heaven to establish His kingdom upon earth; and thus what was contingent and particular in the historical beginning became idealised and universalised by being fitted as a completing member into the frame of the universal revelation of God as it advanced through universal history. And on the other hand, the metaphysical conception of the Logos as immanent in the world, and ordering it according to law, was filled with religious and moral contents; and thus by its connection with the person of the founder of the historical Church, the Logos, from being a cosmical principle of nature, became a religious principle of salvation, the ideal of the good which is present and active in the community, the personified idea of the man who came from God and who is united with God. Thus in the Christian Idea of God these two sides have been combined from the beginning — the moral-religious ideal of the anthropomorphically represented holy Lord and merciful Father—which ideal sprang from the prophetic and apostolic preaching; and the metaphysical principle, which sprang from the Greek speculation of the infinite Spirit exalted above all human limitation, the ground of the existence and of the order of the universe, in whom we live and move and have our being. To mediate internally these two sides of the Christian idea of God was the problem of the Patristic theology, and it also lies at the basis of the formulæ of the doctrine of the Trinity, in which we can see the attempt to connect the Greek and Jewish cognition of God in a higher synthesis, and to guard against all deviations to the one side or the other.

For the mediation of these two sides the whole further history of Christian theology and philosophy has laboured, and naturally the one side has come into the foreground at one time, and the other at another. The Greek fathers, especially the Alexandrians Clement and Origen, emphasised the absolute spirituality of God in opposition not merely to all heathen and gnostic Naturalism, but also to the Jewish Anthropomorphism. According to the profound theologian Clement, God is incognisable as regards His essence in Itself, because

He is elevated above all finite properties; but He is cognisable according to His revelation in the Logos as the principle both of the natural order of the world and also of the historical religious institution of salvation. On the other hand, Tertullian, a father of the Western Church, could not think of God realistically and humanly enough, so much so that he had even no hesitation is ascribing a body to God, seeing that, as he thought, there is nothing actual that is incorporeal. A remarkable combination of the two sides referred to is contained in the theology of the great Church father Augustine. From the Neo-Platonic standpoint with which he began, he taught the abstract simplicity of the divine essence, in which all qualities are annulled into an indifference, so that one can more easily say what God is *not* than what He *is*. Yet the three fundamental determinations—absolute being, knowing, and loving—are predicated of God; but these, again, are identical with each other. As absolute Being and Knowing, God, according to Augustine, who in this follows Plato, is the "eternal truth," the ground and goal of our knowing; as Love, He is the "unchangeable good," the true object of our willing in so far as we are determined to His fellowship, and can therefore find no satisfaction in any finite good. If these determinations in some measure already go beyond the presupposed absolute simplicity of the divine essence, there cannot be brought at all into accordance with it what Augustine has taught concerning the double decree of God, or His will of election and reprobation. It is the Jewish Monotheism which breaks forth in this hard representation of God's judicial attitude towards the fall of Adam, and in so glaring a manner as could hardly have been considered possible in the case of a disciple of Plato. Nevertheless, Augustine, with the two sides of his contradictory doctrine of God, became none the less authoritative for the ecclesiastical theology; and not only for the medieval theology, but also for the Protestant theology, which has never liberated itself from this contradiction which lies within its doctrine of God.

In the Middle Ages the monistic (metaphysical) idea of God had remained limited to individual mystic-speculative thinkers (Scotus Erigena, Meister Eckart, the author of the 'German Theology'). The same idea was carried out in the seventeenth century with great boldness by Spinoza. In opposition to all anthropomorphic Theism, he taught that God is the only independent self-existing being, or the absolute substance which presents itself to our thinking under the two fundamental forms of reality as Thinking and Extension, and out of which all things and souls proceed with purposeless necessity as the finite modes of the manifestation (*modi*) of its infinite being. This doctrine did not deserve the objection of Atheism which has been often advanced against it; it might much rather be called Akosmism, as it appears to merge the reality of the finite in the one substance of the infinite. But its serious weakness is the total lack of the conception of purpose or end, whereby a fatalistic and naturalistic character threatens to come into this Pantheism, which becomes fatal to the religious consciousness. If everything proceeds with the same necessity from God, and if there is not a development from lower to higher modes of existence, if all that happens is only causally conditioned and not guided by final causes nor striving after ends,—then, along with all the other distinctions of worth, the moral distinctions also fall away; the Idea of the Good, the ideal of what ought to be, becomes fiction and illusion, and there remains nothing more for man but to renounce all and every moral ideal, and the highest moral ideals, and to submit to the unchangeable necessity of being and event. Of this nature also is the piety to which, according to Spinoza, we are to attain through our knowing the order of the world as conformable to law. But as certainly as spiritual elevation belongs to religion, just as certain is it that such elevation as we find in Spinoza's system is not yet really religious. For elevation presupposes an ideal which stands above reality, and hence a God can never satisfy the religious consciousness who, like the God of Spinoza, would only be the ground of being and not also of the being that-ought-to-be,—who would be only the highest truth for the theoretical spirit and not also the highest good for the moral spirit. But notwithstanding this, it cannot be denied that Spinoza's struggle against the popular anthropomorphic representation of God as a limited individual Being, who pursues His own particular purposes according to caprice and arbitrariness, was well founded. He thereby emphasised with great resoluteness a side of the religious Idea of God which is but too easily forgotten in the popular religion, but in doing so he fell into the opposite one-sidedness.

'To the Pantheism of Spinoza Leibnitz opposed the Theistic conception of God. God is, according to Leibnitz, the founder of the harmony of all individual beings or monads, which, being without connection in themselves, have been brought only by God into that ordered connection whereby they form the best of all possible worlds. Hence God must be thought of as the perfect ideal of our own souls; wisdom, power, and goodness, which we have in part, are whole in Him. As the perfect ideal, He is for us at the same time the object of the love that gives happiness, which recognises what is truly best in the will of God, and serves Him joyfully in obedience and devotion. The cheerful optimism of Leibnitz's view of the world rests essentially upon the conviction that the world is the work of the infinite wisdom and goodness of God. But although this belief in God ruled the century of the *Aufklärung*, nevertheless it could not permanently satisfy; the synthesis of the good and true was reached too easily, so that neither of the two sides obtained its full right—*i.e.*, neither the unconditionedness of the moral ideal, nor the infinitude of the metaphysical ground of the world. And hence we see at the end of the eighteenth century the tendencies separating again on both sides. Lessing, Herder and Goethe, Schelling and Schleiermacher went back to Spinozism, but sought to connect it with the Leibnitzian individualism, and to animate it in the sense of a teleological development of the world. Kant, on the other hand, declared the metaphysical idea of God to be incognisable, and held exclusively to the postulate of the moral Lawgiver, Judge, and Ruler of the world, to believe in whom reason felt itself compelled, because only under this assumption could it be tranquillised regarding the realisability of the highest good. Fichte transformed the Kantian postulate of a moral Orderer of the world into the faith in the moral world-order, which does not need to be grounded upon a personal God, seeing that it is itself the ultimate and the unconditionally certain. Hegel demanded that Spinoza's substance should be conceived as subject, as the living world-spirit which moves by the Dialectic of the absolute thinking through all the forms and stages of being, which externalises itself in Nature, which comes to itself in Man, and which realises itself in the historical development of the human spirit as a kingdom of truth and freedom. This was a renovation of the Leibnitzian optimism, only with the distinction that with Leibnitz it is the wisdom of a personal Creator that foreordains ("pre-establishes") the harmony of the world, whereas with Hegel it is the universal thinking ("the Idea") identical with being, which unfolds itself by logical necessity into the organism of the world, and which therefore is nothing else through and through but the manifestation of the Idea, the self-actualisation of the divine reason. In this "Panlogism," as the Hegelian philosophy has not been inaptly called, it however appeared that the actual existence of reality did not attain to its full right in two respects. If everything actual is rational, as Hegel said, where then remains the evil and badness of the world? Does not its existence appear rather to point to an irrational ground of the world? So asked Schopenhauer; and he therefore put in the place of the absolute reason the reasonless "Will," or blind impulse of life as the ground of the world, which just on that account is so irrational, so full of evil and suffering,—as Schopenhauer proceeded to show in detail, attaching himself to the Indian pessimism, and with many a dash of cynical irony. The defect of the Hegelian Panlogism was found in another respect in this, that there is no place for individual existence, for the right of the individual or of personality, in a world which presents only a system of categories, determinations of thought, or conceptions, and in which therefore only the universal is real. Hence the Leibnitzian individualism was then revived by philosophers like Herbart and Lotze; they emphasised the worth of personality, and thought of God as the ideal or absolute personality, which, however, according to Lotze, is not to be considered as standing dualistically in opposition to the world, but as including the world in Himself in a way analogous to that in which our spirit includes in itself the totality of its representations. Finally, the powerful advance of the natural sciences in our century has had as its consequence in Germany that the Idealism which since Kant, and even since Leibnitz, had there its home, has been given up by many, at least for the theoretical view of the world, and an Atheistic Realism has been put into its place—either as Materialism, Atomism, Hylozoism, or as Scepticism, Phenomenalism, Positivism. But at the same time many upholders of theoretical Materialism or Naturalism have nevertheless maintained the right of Idealism in the sphere of the practical view of life. Feuerbach, David Strauss, Albert Lange, have been the leaders of a widespread school which holds the Idea of God to be indeed a fiction and illusion, but whose adherents yet hold fast to the moral ideal of the good as the final end of human life and of history. Here the question necessarily arises, how the good can be the purpose or end of the world if it is not also in some sense the basis of the world? And hence we stand once more before the old and eternal problem of the belief in God, which has just for its object the synthesis of the true and the good, or of the real principle of the world and the moral ideal of the human heart.

This analysis of the Idea of God into its two constituent elements has been presented lately in a peculiarly instructive way in the controversy between Herbert Spencer and the Comtean positivist Frederic Harrison. The former comes through analysis of the real world to the acceptance of an absolute reality, or an infinite and eternal power, which must be presupposed as the background and bearer of all that is relative and phenomenal, but whose qualities and relation to phenomena are for us unknowable. This unknowable absolute is, according to Spencer, just the object of religion, the great mystery, in the worship of which all religions are at one. According to the positivist, on the other hand, such an absolute being is not existent, at least for us, and can have no significance whatever either for our religious feeling or for our scientific thinking; it is rather Humanity that ought to be the object of the religious feeling,—to it we should feel ourselves bound through grateful piety, and we should bind ourselves to its service in devoted benevolence. On the one side, therefore, we have a supreme moral ideal without a metaphysical ground; on the other, an ultimate metaphysical principle without a final moral purpose; and on either side we have the one half of what as a whole forms the content of the belief in God. Shall this *antithesis* be the last word? Or will it not rather be the preparation for a *deeper synthesis*, a purer apprehension of that belief which is inalienable, because indispensable to humanity —the belief in the God of whom, through whom, and to whom are all things, to whom be glory for ever, Amen.

LECTURE V.

THE REVELATION OF GOD IN THE NATURAL ORDER OF THE WORLD.

It may be accepted as a recognised position that, since the criticism of Hume and Kant, the so-called proofs of the existence of God can no longer be maintained in their common scholastic form. No one holds it still to be possible to prove the existence of God from an abstract conception of God, by means of a process of inference, or from an abstract conception of the world to infer its cause in a God separated from it. But, from the fact that the old scholastic demonstrations no longer hold good, it would, however, be very precipitate to conclude that the question regarding the truth of the belief in God cannot be an object of our reflection at all. However often this question may be put aside, it will, nevertheless, always press itself again upon the human mind as the greatest problem for its thought. And especially in the present day, when the bases of religion appear to be wavering in so many ways, it has become a more burning question than ever. But if it be said that it is unnecessary that we should trouble ourselves to prove God's existence, seeing that He Himself does in fact prove Himself to us by His living revelation which He permits us to experience, then we reply that this is just the very problem at issue—namely, how to demonstrate the revelation of God in human experience; how to bring it to the consciousness of men, to awaken the understanding and interest for it in the doubters and the indifferent, and then to obtain from the manifold revelations in the different spheres of life the corresponding expressions regarding the divine government and being. This was just the sum and substance of what was always meant and aimed at in the "Demonstrations of God" in the earlier examples of them. They were designed to point out the way by which mankind came to the consciousness of God by the reflecting understanding; and to show, from the analysis of human experience, the justification, the good ground, and meaning of the belief in God. In order to avoid misunderstandings which cling to the term "Proofs" or "Demonstrations," we therefore rather say that our task is to describe the revelation of God in the Natural, Moral, and Religious Order of the World. And to-day we shall be occupied in the first place with the *Natural World-Order*, which is related to the moral and religious Order of the World, as the universal is to the particular, and to the most particular; or as the base of the pyramid is to its middle and apex. On each of these stages of the Order of the World we have to distinguish a subjective and an objective side, a world of consciousness and of existence, which correspond to each other in such a manner that neither side can be understood without reference to the other. It is just in this reciprocal relatedness and orderedness of the two to each other that the one single ordering principle of the whole reveals itself; and this principle is God. It is of importance to recognise this double-sidedness of the Order of the World, because thereby the attempt, which has been often recently made, to put the Order of the World itself in the place of God, is excluded from the outset. For a conception, which when more exactly examined resolves itself into a duality of correlative conceptions, cannot possibly be the highest concluding Idea; but it certainly contains the unfolding and manifestation of the One in the many, the revelation of God in the world of internal and external experience.

When the "Natural Order of the World" is spoken of, we usually think only of the order of external Nature, as a whole of things and effects, which exist independent of our thinking. But David Hume has already shown that the radical conceptions of substantiality and causality, by means of which we think the ordered world, are not given to us from without, but are added by our own thought to the impressions of the senses. Thereafter Kant taught that the forms of perception and thought, by means of which we connect the sensations into ideas and judgments, originally belong to our mind, and he has accordingly called our understanding on that account "the Legislator of Nature"—that is to say, of the Nature represented by us, and which forms the content of our consciousness. In fact, it cannot be disputed that the world of which we know immediately is just the world of our consciousness, which at all events rests primarily upon the functions and laws of our mind. Hence the question immediately arises, Is there corresponding to this our subjective world of consciousness, also an objective world of existence independent of our consciousness, or is there not? If this question is affirmed, we then stand before the cardinal question of the theory of knowledge, How the agreement of our thought-world with the real world, upon which the truth of our knowledge rests, is thinkable? This question is simply evaded by the subjective idealism which denies a real world and only accepts the thought-world of our consciousness.

Although this idealistic way of thinking has in our day not very many representatives, we will yet try to transfer ourselves hypothetically, for a moment, to its standpoint. Now so much at all events is clear, that even the idealist, if he would not fall into the absurdity of "Solipsism," must at least accept a plurality of subjects of consciousness which stand related to one another in the exchange of thoughts, through the medium of language. But then, it is asked, how do these different minds come to the harmonious representation of a nature common to them, and that is the medium of their reciprocal action? To this Fichte has answered, that the agreement of finite minds in the notion of an external world is explained by the fact that they are only the limited forms of the manifestation of a universal reason. In a similar sense Berkeley had already said that the idea of external things is produced in human minds by God. But if any one perhaps preferred to say that the similarity in the human representations of an external nature is explained by the similar psychological laws of our process of representation, the question would thereby only be driven further back. For whence, we must then necessarily ask, this similarity of the psychological processes and states, if the individual minds were originally separate independent monads, and were not bound to each other by a universal consciousness that embraced all the individuals? If, in accordance with a logical individualism, we hold every individual Ego to be a monad which shuts itself up in its own ideal world, and that its representations flow on independently of any universal spiritual principle, then the agreement in the representations of the individual Egos regarding the common world surrounding them would be an inconceivable mystery. And, moreover, we can no longer speak of error and truth in the representations of each individual, because there would be no universal criterion by which to judge them; the course of the representations of every individual consciousness would then be just as true as that of every other, and the movement of the waking consciousness would be no more true than that of one who dreamed. In short, there would be in this intellectual anarchy, as such, no longer any truth or any order, or a Cosmos, but only a Chaos of many associations of ideas, running on side by side. Therefore, even in the hypothetically assumed case, that there is only an ideal nature in the consciousness of thinking minds, we could not escape from the question how the different subjects come to a corresponding image of the world, and how they are able to distinguish what is merely subjectively represented, from the common or objective mode of representation—that is to say, how they can distinguish error from truth. This question, however, can hardly be solved otherwise than by the assumption of a universal consciousness, which must be the common ground, as well as the ruling law, of all individual consciousnesses or minds.

But we are not able seriously to appropriate or hold the hypothesis of subjective idealism. How high soever we may think of our spiritual life as elevated above external Nature, we cannot, however, establish such an absolute gulf between the two that reality should only pertain to the former and not to the latter. We cannot shut out the consideration that a life nearly related to human consciousness is also found in the sub-human world among the lower animals; and how then can we deny them real existence? And, besides, seeing that there are only graduated distinctions existing between the animal and the vegetable manifestations, and again between the latter and the minerals, no reason can be seen why a real existence by itself can be denied to any one part of the phenomena which we call "Nature." The view which is self-evident to the sound human understanding, that with all our consciousness of the world there corresponds a real world existing by itself independent of our thinking, is certainly not merely the simplest but also the most correct hypothesis for the explanation of the facts of our consciousness. Wherein "naïve Realism"—the realism of common-sense—errs, and requires and needs justification by philosophical reflection, is only in the opinion that the world of reality as existing in itself entirely corresponds to the world represented by us, and that the latter is only a passively received copy of the former. This error has been refuted by the critical analysis of the process of cognition showing that we build up our world of consciousness self-actively out of the raw material of sensations, by means of the forms of perception and thinking that are innate in us. The truth which we are accustomed to ascribe to this world of consciousness cannot indeed consist in its being the exact copy of a world of reality that has just the same colours and sounds belonging to it; but the truth lies properly in this, that the subjectively conditioned images of our consciousness contain the representative signs, by which we know the relations of real existences to each other and to us. As the letters of a writing are the written signs by means of which we are able to reproduce the thoughts of the author, so the representations and associations of representation in our consciousness are the sign-language by means of which we reproduce the relations of things to one another and to ourselves, or make the real world an object of our knowledge. And thus arises the question which has been already indicated, namely, How is it possible that our connection of sensations into representations and of representations into judgments, which *we ourselves* carry on according to *our subjective* forms of perception and thinking, is the correct sign and correlative of real things and of their relations, as they are *in themselves* independent of our representing of them? This correspondence between the world thought by us, and the real world as it exists in itself, upon which all the truth of our knowing rests, appears to me only explicable on the assumption that the Order of the Real World is subject to analogous laws of being and working, as the Order of our Ideal World is to laws of perceiving and thinking.

That it actually is so, is, in the first place, a postulate of our theoretical reason, without which we should be compelled entirely to despair of all truth in our knowing. But we also have a proof of the correctness of this postulate in daily experience as often as we see results, which were expected on the grounds of the laws of Nature as thought by us, correctly appear. For example, the astronomer may calculate a future celestial phenomenon, on the basis of the laws of the motions of the heavenly bodies, which he has nowhere deciphered in the heavens, but which his own understanding has thought out in order by means of them to explain and arrange the Chaos of the manifold terrestrial phenomena. If, then, the phenomenon calculated by him presents itself punctually at the minute to his perception, this is manifestly a proof of the correctness of the laws thought out by the astronomer—*i.e.*, a proof of their agreement with the laws according to which the heavenly bodies actually move. Hence the laws according to which the human understanding thinks and calculates, arranges the given phenomena and anticipates future ones, correspond to the laws according to which things hang together and work upon each other in the real world. How is this correspondence between the laws of our thinking, which are not given to us from without, and the laws of being, which are not made by us, explained? So far as I see, only from this, that the two have their common ground in a

Divine thinking, in a creative Reason which manifests its thoughts partly in the Order of the real world and partly in the thinking of our understanding as it copies that Order. The agreement of our thinking with the being of the world rests on the fact that it is the reproduction of the creative thoughts of the Infinite mind, a reproduction which is always imperfect according to the measure of the finite mind. The truth of our cognition is a participating in *the* truth which God essentially is.

This is the proper sense and the abiding truth contained in the so-called "Ontological Argument," the tenor of which refers to the relation of thinking and being so understood. This argument is as old as religious reflection. It is already contained in the words of the Psalmist, "In Thy light we see light." It forms the hinge of the philosophy of Plato, according to which the highest Idea, or God, is the ground both of knowing and of being, and all true cognition is a participation in the world of the Ideas of the Divine reason. In like manner, according to Augustine, God is the eternal truth, the ground and goal of all the true thinking of man. According to Thomas Aquinas, we see and judge all things in the light of God, in so far as the natural light of our reason is a participating in the Divine light. In the hands of Anselm this thought, which is distinctly found exhibited in his 'Proslogium,' received the unfortunate scholastic turn, that from the conception of God as the most perfect Being, an inference is drawn of His existence as one of the attributes contained in the conception. This inference, which is also found repeated by Descartes and Wolff, has been rightly disposed of by Kant as a piece of school wit; but his criticism shot beyond the mark and overlooked the deeper correct thought, which is concealed under the deceptive scholastic form of the ontological argument. Kant, in setting up such an opposition between Thinking and Being as that no way led from the former to the latter at all, makes not merely the Being of God, but likewise that of the world, unknowable. Knowledge being separated from Being, is limited to mere subjective phenomena, and is consequently at bottom robbed of all truth. The philosophy of Hegel reacted against this exaggerated dualism, but it fell again, in its turn, into just as exaggerated a monism in simply identifying Thinking and Being. Thereby the problem of the theory of Knowledge was not so much solved as rather cut in pieces by the sword, and the distinction between the real creative thinking of God and our ideally reproductive thinking was so confounded, that Strauss and Feuerbach were able to draw from it the absurd consequence of explaining the human thinking itself as the absolute self-deification of speculative philosophy, a view which soon enough was bitterly revenged by its passing into materialism. The point of the "Ontological" argument lies rather just in this, that our

Thinking and Being are indeed different, yet are constituted for each other by the conformity of the laws on both sides, and that in this agreement—or pre-established harmony, according to Leibnitz—of the two sides, the unity of the ordering principle, *i.e.* of the effectuating Thinking or the Omnipotent Reason of God, reveals itself.

In our consideration of the Natural Order of the World we started from its ideal side, or the side of consciousness. The result found in this relation will be completed and confirmed if we now also consider it from the real side. In doing so we come to the subject of the " Cosmological " and " Teleological " arguments. Kant's criticism has shown on philosophical grounds that these two arguments are untenable in their traditional scholastic form, and these grounds are further strengthened by the Natural Science of the present day. The " Cosmological" argument reasoned from the contingency of the world to its having been produced by a necessary extra-mundane cause; and the well-founded objection has been raised against it by Hume and Kant that the argument starts from an arbitrary view, for, from the fact that every individual thing in the world is a contingent thing—*i.e.*, is conditioned by something else—it does not at all follow that the same relation holds good of the world as a whole,—that it is contingent, and must have its ground in an extra-mundane cause. It is not the contingency, but the universal and constant conformity of nature to law, that is the fundamental presupposition of the science of the present day — a presupposition which certainly cannot be proved, but which must be accepted if there is to be an inductive investigation of Nature, and which is always confirmed anew by every step in the advance of our knowledge of Nature, so that its probability approaches certainty. But because we in the present day know Nature as a connected order of causes and effects better than former ages knew it, shall the words of the apostle on that account be less valid for us, that " the invisible things of God from the creation of the world are clearly seen, being understood by the things that are made, even His eternal power and Godhead " ? (Rom. i. 20.)

If we hold Nature to be a system of forces which stand in regulated reciprocal action with each other, the ultimate riddle of the universe is thereby so far from being solved that the question rather first arises, How, then, is a causal working of one being upon another at all to be explained ? The popular statement, that an influence passes from the one to the other, is an image which can explain nothing; for the state which has appeared through a change in the first thing cannot leave this thing and pass over to a second or third thing, and so on, but it has only as a consequence that in the second thing, the third thing, and so on, corresponding states also appear. What we call the causal working of things upon each other consists in this, that upon an alteration in the one thing corresponding alterations necessarily follow in the other things. This, however, as Lotze has luminously shown, would be inconceivable under the supposition that the individual things are independent existences and were indifferent towards each other; it becomes conceivable, however, on the view that they are embraced as parts or members in an all-comprehending living unity. For then the alteration in a part is at the same time an alteration in the state of the whole, and accordingly calls forth the alteration in another part as its completing compensation. If, therefore, the mystery of transeunt causality is solved by this, that we refer it to the immanent causality within an organic whole, we come to see in the regulated reciprocity of the individual forces, or in "Nature," the manifestation of a single primary force or "Omnipotence" which unfolds itself in an infinite multiplicity of mutually related effects.

But how shall we now have to think more precisely of this primary force? Are we to conceive of it as a material and blindly working force, or as a spiritual and intelligent power? The deciding grounds for answering this question will indeed only be shown in consideration of the moral and religious World Order in the next lecture; yet, even upon the standpoint of our present more general consideration, certain grounds may be recognised which speak for the spiritual character of the principle of the Order of Nature. Let us first of all recall to mind whence our conception of an efficient force is derived. It cannot be given to us from without, for what we immediately perceive are only changing phenomena; if we see in them effects of forces, this is already an interpretation which we derive from the analogy of the effects produced by ourselves. The only force or power which we know immediately and from within, is the power of our own will; from its working, its being checked, and its counter-working, arises originally our conception of efficient power, and therefore of causality generally. By this we are assuredly justified in thinking of the universal cause which lies at the basis of all particular things, according to the analogy of the power of the will which is alone immediately known to us, and consequently to think it as a spiritual principle. Likewise the constant regularity with which things so work upon each other that there exists an Order, a constant unity, in the multiplicity of the processes changing in time, could hardly otherwise be explained than according to psychological analogy—namely, by the supposition that the mode of the working of the manifold forces is determined by thoughts, which have their unity in the thinking of the Divine will that governs the world. As in us it is the thinking reason which comprises the multiplicity of the changing phenomena of consciousness under conceptions and laws, and which connects them into an ordered image of the world, so we may behold in the corresponding order of the real world the unfolding of the thoughts of the creative reason of God. If this analogical inference were not justified, neither should we have any right to hold the view that there is a real Order of the World, corresponding to the Order of the World thought by us, and consequently we should have no right to ascribe objective truth to our thinking. That we think causally—*i.e.*, connect Cause and Effect by a super-temporal logical necessity—presupposes that in the real world Cause and Effect also hang together through an equally logical necessity, which cannot be grounded in the temporal phenomena but only in the supra-temporal logical principle which rules over and combines them. In short, the logical truth of the principle of the sufficient reason presupposes that the ground and law of the temporal phenomena lie in a Divine Logos.

But our thinking is as essentially teleological as causal; both are grounded on the same original experience in ourselves. For the alterations which we evoke in external states by the exercise of our will have been, before they appeared, already present to us in more or less clear consciousness, as internally represented objects or ends of our activity. Along with the conception of causality there arises to us, therefore, out of the same experience of our own activity, also at the same time, that of purpose or end; the two are only different modes of contemplating the same process. Hence the connection of the two modes of contemplating things is inherently so natural and inevitable that we only learn gradually to separate the two more definitely, but we are never able to dispense entirely with either of them. It was so natural for religious reflection to see a revelation of the divine reason in the positiveness of Nature, that we are not surprised when we meet with this mode of contemplation in the earliest antiquity. Kant rightly called the Teleological Argument the oldest, the clearest, and the best adapted to the common reason, and he says that it always deserves to be mentioned with respect. The objections which he raises to it rather strike the popular anthropomorphic form of the argument than its proper kernel. So far as the argument only proceeds from the form of things as purposively arranged, it brings us, Kant said, to a mere author of this form, an Architect of the world, and not a Creator of the world. And as experience, nevertheless, shows us no unlimited purposiveness, but much that is contrary to design in detail, the inference of a perfect designing intelligence is not justified,—certainly a very noteworthy objection to the popular apprehension of the argument, in which the conclusion drawn proceeds from the artificial constitution of the world to an extra-mundane Creator of perfect wisdom and unconditioned power. But the main question is, whether this whole way of viewing the subject is at all correct? To represent the world as an artificial machine, and God as the skilful maker of it, might indeed appear natural to the mechanical way of thinking prevalent in the seventeenth and eighteenth centuries; but to us of the present day this representation has become strange and impossible to be thought. Since Herder and Goethe, we have learned to see in Nature not a made work of Art but a living organism whose life is unfolded and formed from within, according to its own impulse and laws. And this way of contemplating Nature, which was already anticipated in genial intuition by the poets and thinkers at the beginning of the century, has received a magnificent confirmation in our age through Darwin's investigation of nature. The theory of development, in its fundamental idea at least, is accepted generally nowadays as one of the most certain conquests of scientific investigation. It is now clear that by it the earlier form of the Teleological Argument has become untenable; for if the living beings have become such as we know them of themselves through natural causes, the question as to an external author through whom they have been made has begun to give way. Yet the opinion, not unfrequently heard, that with the theory of development the conception of purpose or end in general, and with it all ideal principles, have been banished from the thinking contemplation of the world, may nevertheless be very precipitate. The teleological way of viewing things, as Kant has already shown in the 'Critique of the Judgment,' is for us as irrefragable a psychological necessity as the causal connection of phenomena. The only question at issue is the correct combination of the two, and for this question the conception of "Development" is of the greatest importance.

The modern Theory of Development appears to me so little to contradict the acceptance of an immanent rational principle of the world, that, when rightly understood, it may rather serve as a powerful support of it. The kernel of this theory, when collateral and disputable determinations are left out of view, will be found in the following two propositions: (1) All the life of the earth is *one* uninterrupted connected process of development, which has reached its goal in man, and from this point the natural process passes over into the historical process; (2) all the forms of life from the lowest to the highest are developed out of simple fundamental forms, under the co-operation of inner vital impulses and external conditions of life. That in the case of some the external conditions of life are more accentuated, and in the case of others the internal vital impulses are more accentuated, may be of important consequence in the application of the theory to investigation in detail, but it nevertheless makes no difference in principle. In Darwin's theory the inner vital impulse is not wanting, however it may appear to retreat behind the external conditions of life ; for what else is the "struggle for existence" but the exercise of the impulse of self-preservation ? Yet the other impulses will not have to be excluded — namely, those which aim at the invigoration, expansion, and perfection of life, according to the tendency determined by its inherent nature. All life effectuates itself in the exercise of impulses which strive after those states in which the living being finds satisfaction, and which therefore correspond to its nature, and promote its preservation and perfectionment. May it not, then, be rightly said, that all life is determined by ends which, although unconscious to the individual being itself, yet as impulse and instinct predetermine from the beginning the direction and the course of the development of its life? And was not, therefore, Aristotle right when he taught that the end is not only the last, but also the first, and the impelling power of the whole movement? But if it holds true of the individual being, that the final end which results from the development of its life is also already the ideal prius of the whole process, then we shall be able to apply the same thought to the whole process of the life of our earth, and to draw therefrom a conclusion as to the principle of this process. And we are justified in doing so by the very fundamental thought of modern biology, according to which all the life of the earth forms *one* advancing development from the lowest to the highest forms of existence. If we survey the whole of this development, we see how with the growing differentiation and refinement of the sensible organisation there comes in at the same time a growing, deepening, and clearing of the psychical life, rising up from the dull sensations of the lowest living beings to the dawning consciousness of the higher animals, and at last to the clear human consciousness, which objectifies its representations in language, and thereby attains and secures the independence of the spiritual life. Shall we not, then, be entitled to draw the conclusion, that this very spiritual life of man has been the end to which the whole process of life on our earth strove from the beginning and constantly through all transformations of the organisation—that it was the final end for which all previous natural existence has been only the preparatory stage, the subservient means, the causal mechanism? But how, we ask, is it to be made intelligible that our earth, which was once on a time a glowing ball, produced life which had spirit as its end, if it were not that this spirit of the life of the earth, in its process of becoming, had its ultimate ground in the eternal spirit of the universal life?—if it had not been the purposive thought of the creative reason of God, which realised itself in the teleological process of the movement of all life in the terrestrial sphere of the world, and indeed in every other sphere as well? As little as biological science can be prevented from searching into the causal conditions and connections of the terrestrial development of life in detail, just as little are we hindered, on the other hand, from seeing in the whole of this causal mechanism the means by which the timeless universal consciousness of the infinite Spirit reproduces itself in that advancing movement in time in which the terrestrial life becomes conscious.

It may be said that this view is just a hypothesis, in contrast to which other hypotheses for the explanation of nature stand with equal right, while none of them all can yet be positively verified. Certainly all theories regarding the ultimate basis of life and of its development are hypothetical, and remain hypothetical to the exact science which is directed to individual phenomena. Yet I think that the hypothesis which has just been presented has the advantage that it admits the right which is claimed for the ideal side of the order of nature, the facts of our consciousness; whereas in the materialistic hypotheses, which see in nature merely the causal mechanism of forces, or matter without spirit and end, the fact of the knowing spirit itself always remains an uncomprehended and incomprehensible riddle. Now, as was said at the beginning of this lecture, if there belong to the whole of the order of nature the two sides—namely, the knowing spirit and the nature that is to be known—then the higher claim to truth may well be admitted to belong to *that* hypothesis which is able to explain, not merely one of the two sides while leaving out the other, but both sides equally, and which can conceive their reciprocal correspondence from the unity of their common ground.

That the scientific consideration of nature, which is directed to the causal conformity of phenomena to law, is not the only justifiable way of regarding it, may be proved even from the daily experience of common life. For the impression of the beautiful which nature makes upon the human mind is quite independent of the intellectual knowledge which relates to causal connection; and it presses itself upon the learned investigator of nature, who perhaps denies all Teleology in principle and all that is Ideal in nature, with the same necessity as on the simple sense of the uneducated man who has never formed any thoughts regarding the grounds of the origin of phenomena, and yet involuntarily feels and admires their sublimity and beauty. Now it is of course said that the impression of the beautiful is a purely subjective feeling, from which no conclusions whatever can be drawn regarding the constitution of nature. This is, indeed, so far correct, that the æsthetic sensation is subjectively conditioned by the disposition, not merely of the senses, but still more of the soul of the individual; and that the æsthetic capacity, like every other, must also be developed and cultivated to a certain degree in order that the individual may receive the impression of the beautiful from nature. And yet it does not follow from this that the sensation of the beautiful is something merely subjective, an arbitrary product of our fantasy, which we groundlessly assign to external nature when we feel our æsthetic sense excited by nature. There must just as certainly be an objective qualification of real nature corresponding to this our subjective sensation, as there are real objects and their relations in the world corresponding to our representations and the connections of our representations. What, then, may that qualification of nature be which we perceive by means of the æsthetic sensation, and which we have accordingly to conceive as the objective correlate of the subjective impression of the beautiful? Kant already pointed out, and the more recent æsthetics have put it into still clearer light, that the modification of nature which is perceived by us as beauty is its immanent purposiveness, the harmonious relation of the parts to the whole, the rational necessity which governs the free play of forces, and which establishes unity in a multiplicity. And hence the teleological ideal background of reality, the shining of the Idea through phenomena, is that which we feel as the beauty of nature; and assuredly we could not feel it if the receptivity for it were not also given in the rational constitution of our soul. In this there is also established that correspondence of the inner and outer, of subjective and objective rationality, which is the ground of all our knowing of the world. We are therefore led from this side of the contemplation of nature again to the same conclusion, that the beauty of nature stands to us as a revelation of the creative spirit, which has also lent us the capacity to recognise the glory of His works, and to imitate it in creating artistic forms.

We have considered the order of nature from its two sides, the Ideal and Real, and have come on both sides to the same harmonious result. We have recognised in it the revelation of *one* principle, which is universal consciousness as well as omnipotence, and which is therefore the revelation of a thinking and willing spirit, or God. But here there arises a difficulty which is too important for us to leave unnoticed. We know thinking and willing only in the form of a human consciousness, to which the limits of finiteness essentially belong. Consciousness is a distinguishing of the knowing subject from the known object to which it stands opposed, and by which it is limited. It does not itself create its material, but finds it presented and given to it. It relates itself passively to the impressions of things, and is therefore dependent on a presented world. In like manner, the will is a form of desire which presupposes a want in the willer, and it directs itself to objects in which it finds the material and means of its activity, and at the same time a restraint of that activity, or a resistance which it has to overcome. All this appears to presuppose a limited individual being which is conditioned and limited by another. How then, it may be asked, can such determination be transferred or assigned to God without making Him finite, or without making Him a man enlarged to gigantic proportions, which is making Him a mythical phantom? Certainly this is a question which requires earnest consideration, which at all events warns us to great caution in the transference of human qualities to the Divine Being. Shall we, then, under the weight of this difficulty, simply desist from speaking of a Thinking and Willing of God? Shall we deny Him conscious spiritual life, and designate Him only as the unconscious soul of the world, or still more indefinitely, as an active force? I fear that if we were to follow this suggestion we should get still further away from the truth, and fall into a still worse error in a practical respect than would be the case in following an uncritical Anthropomorphism.

The self-conscious and self-determining life of man is unquestionably the highest form of life which we know at all. Now if it be admitted that in the case of man it is confined to the limit of finitude, and cannot in this human finite form find place in God, yet it does not yet follow from this that we must deny to God the highest that we know from our experience. As there cannot lie less in the cause than in the effect, nor less in the whole than in the part, the infinite principle of the world, which produces the human spirit along with all else and embraces them in itself, cannot possess the spiritual energy of life in less measure, but rather in a much more perfect degree, than man. But what gives the self-conscious spirit of man its peculiar prerogative above the sub-human life is not the side of finiteness which it has in common with the latter, but that *self-activity* of the Ego, which distinguishes itself as the permanent and governing unity, from the manifold and changing contents of consciousness, and which even thereby raises itself above dependence on the matter presented to it, and lowers it to the position of a means serving its free self. The usual opinion that self-consciousness is only the distinguishing of the Ego from the non-Ego is not correct; rather is the self-consciousness primarily and essentially a distinguishing of itself from itself—that is to say, of the abiding and combining unity of the self from the plurality and mutability of its contents. So also the will is not primarily a desire that is directed to external things; but it is self-determination—*i.e.*, determination of the manifold divided expressions of life, by the unity of the thinking which posits ends to itself. Now it is incontestably true that consciousness and will in the case of man presuppose a given material, and therefore the fact on the one hand of their being conditioned by another, or of passivity and finiteness; but it is not less certain on the other hand that just that which distinguishes the human spirit from the sub-human life—namely, its self-consciousness and its self-determination—does not consist essentially of passivity, but of the spontaneity of the Ego as existing by itself, which in the changing of its elements asserts itself as the persistent and governing unity of that which is manifold and changeable. This free self-activity which unfolds its inner unity into a multiplicity of living forms and states, in the act of distinguishing itself, abides with itself, and makes itself actually into that which it is in itself potentially: this is the spiritual being of man by which he rises over all merely finite and conditioned existence, and has a certain, although still weak, participation in that infiniteness and unconditionedness which is original and perfect only in God. What, then, can hinder us from thinking these qualities, which constitute the prerogative of the human mind over spiritless nature, as being posited in God in a perfect manner without their human limit? Why should we not accept something analogous to the human spirit in God, a self-distinguishing of His single and eternal unchangeable Self from the plurality and changeableness of His operations, which form the world of divided temporal phenomena? Without accepting this view it would be difficult to escape from the pantheistic opinion, that the unity of God resolves itself into the coexistence of phenomena in space and their succession in time, so that we can no longer find in Him what we sought in Him—namely, the connecting and ruling power of the world-order. If there is "a resting pole in the flight of phenomena" not merely in our representations but in truth, in being itself, we shall have to seek it in the living spirit of God, who asserts Himself as the independent and permanent Lord of the changing phenomena—as "King of the Æons"—by this, that He distinguishes in His thinking, His eternal inner essence from His changeable working in the world. If the world is an order of events happening according to law and purpose, it is the revelation of an ordering Spirit, who governs the becoming or process of the world with His eternal thoughts, and who therefore is not Himself merged in its process, but knows and effectuates Himself as eternally the same, in distinction from the temporal beings of the world. It is certainly not to be denied that we cannot form a representation of the infinite Spirit whose life is pure self-activity without any conditionedness and dependence, because that transcends all analogy of our experience. But what follows from this? Mayhap that the thought of the unconditioned spirit, because not representable in the mind, is also not true?

Certainly not; for the principle of the world is assuredly not representable, under whatever categories we may attempt it. Yet according to what has been previously adduced, what corresponds best to the need which our thinking has to recognise in the principle of the world the sufficient ground of the order of the world, is the category of the thinking spirit which knows and determines itself; and accordingly we are entitled to hold the view that it is this very category which is most fitted for the designation of the divine essence, and which comes nearest the truth. But what certainly follows from the unrepresentableness of the infinite Spirit is the warning that we are not to attempt to make an image to ourselves of the inner life of God, according to human analogy. All the questions which refer to the inner nature of God, whether it be to His hidden decrees, or to the way in which the existence of the world is reflected in His inner being, or to how His eternal essence is related to the succession of time —whether there is also in Him a remembering and a foreseeing, or whether to Him all is eternally the same present, without past and future,—all such and similar questions pass entirely beyond the limits of our knowledge. In order to be able to answer them we should necessarily have to possess God's omniscience. Here the words of Scripture hold true, "My thoughts are not your thoughts; for as high as the heavens are above the earth, so high are my thoughts above your thoughts." How often have these words been forgotten by theologians and philosophers, who have had the hardihood in their titanic Gnosticism to analyse the inmost nature of Deity, and to mete it out in their formulæ! As a reaction against this arrogant Gnosticism, the faint-hearted Agnosticism of the present day has a relative justification. It is, in fact, true that we are able to know God only so far as He has revealed Himself to us through His working in the whole order of the world, and still continually so reveals Himself. That beyond this side which is turned to us, this being of God for us, there lies beyond another inner side in the being of God for Himself, is a position which has been established to us as true by all that has been said above. But to try to know anything more closely concerning the *What* and *How* of this being of God for Himself, to embrace it in conceptions, to picture it in images,—this we ought never to presume to do. By doing so we should inevitably fall into mythological fantasies which would draw down the Holy mystery of the Godhead into the common distinctness of earthly things, and put empty fabrications in place of the true revelation of God in the order of the world,—fictions which would have as little value for the religious consciousness of the present day as the myths of the Gnostics had in the second century. If those who deny consciousness and personality to God mean only thereby to say that we cannot think of God as affected with human limitations, there would be nothing to object to that position. But the designations "*un*conscious," "*im*personal," may but too easily lead to the misunderstanding that the divine being were less spiritual, consequently more imperfect, than the human; and against this we must decidedly protest. This misunderstanding would, however, be avoided by using the expressions "*super*conscious," "*super*personal," and accordingly I would hold this to be an incontestable formula, in which all those who are convinced of the ideal spiritual essence of the principle of the world might perhaps unite.

With this view the ecclesiastical doctrine is found to be in essential agreement; for, as is well known, the teachers of the Church from the outset, in their determination of the divine attributes, have striven so earnestly to strip off the human limits that very little of the human analogy remains. But the Church has undoubtedly always failed to draw the necessary conclusions from these her correct principles. While her theologians accentuated in the strictest way the timeless unchangeableness of God, they yet represented His omnipotence as revealing itself now in the order of the world, and again without and contrary to it as miracle-working arbitrariness. And thereby they left the door open to the popular anthropomorphism, with all the adjuncts of the belief in miracles and magic. To remove this inconsequence, which has run through the ecclesiastical system of doctrine since the time of Augustine, is a pressing task of our time. It lies as much in the interest of the moral purity of the faith as of the scientific knowledge of the world, that the abstract supra-naturalism of the popular conception of divine omnipotence — that inheritance of Christianity from the Jewish and heathen ways of thinking — should be at last overcome, and the insight disseminated that God is Spirit, infinite Spirit, who as such reveals Himself in the whole of the rational order of the world, according to law and purpose, to which order also the inviolable conformity of nature to law belongs. It is not in the occasional interruption and disturbance of the regulated order by individual miracles, but in the constant regularity, purposiveness, and beauty of nature, that we have to find the sublime revelation of the Eternal Spirit, who, according to the words of Holy Scripture, is a "God of Order," and who has wisely ordered all His works. "The heavens declare the glory of God; and the firmament showeth His handywork."

LECTURE VI.

THE REVELATION OF GOD IN THE MORAL AND RELIGIOUS ORDER OF THE WORLD.

THE order of the world of Nature, as we saw in the last Lecture, is not to be understood, if it is contemplated either only from the point of view of the Ego, or only from that of presented things or objects. In the former case one reaches only a world of thoughts but not the real world; in the latter case the ideal or spiritual constituent, which lies in the conception of the *Order* of the World, remains inexplicable, and that order is resolved into a chaos of unconceived positive data. The essence of the order of nature consists rather in the correlation of the thinking Ego and the thinkable connection of things, a correlation in which we found the very revelation of the creative reason as the highest unity of thinking and being. And exactly the same holds true in regard to the moral and religious order of the world. It, too, is only to be understood if we keep in view the subjective and objective side—the personal consciousness of the world and the historical community of the peoples and religions, in their constant reciprocal relation to each other, and their conditionedness through one another. In this very correlation, this reciprocal tie between the personal conscience and moral society, mankind have always recognised the revelation of a universal or divine will combining the two with each other. It is obvious that we no longer regard this divine grounding of the moral order in the mythological manner prevalent in the childhood of mankind—namely, as a direct divine proclamation of laws given as on Sinai, or enunciated by divine oracles as at Delphi. We have long since learned that human history proceeds everywhere naturally. But it is asked whether the explanation of the moral law would be already exhaustively given, if we only gave heed to the external process through which the moral practices and laws form and alter themselves from motives of utility and of selfish interests; and whether there is not also here concealed under the mechanism of the natural motives a moral idea, a higher teleological order, which betrays its transcendental origin in the unconditionedness of the feeling of duty?

I have already, in the second of these Lectures, attempted to show that the characteristic of the moral feeling is not explained but denied, when it is made a mere product of society led by egoistic interests. It is indeed true that our moral consciousness develops itself only in reciprocity with society, that it receives its definite contents, its knowledge of what is to be regarded as right or wrong, in detail, primarily from the moral practices and tenets of society. But what the distinction of right and wrong generally indicates—namely, that right raises an unconditioned claim to our obedience, that it puts our will internally under obligation quite apart from external consequences—this we could only have learned by instruction from others, unless we had had in our rational constitution by nature the "Moral Sense"—that is, the capacity and the impulse for the judging and ordering of our manifold relations and motives, according to their relative value for the rational purpose of the whole. The "Conscience" is certainly not a sum of innate ideas, a code of law born in us, for in that case the mutability and manifoldness of the moral opinions of men could not possibly be explained. But just as little is the conscience merely a copy of the moral practices and tenets of society that have become actual at any time, for then the unconditionedness of its obligatory and judicial authority would be inexplicable. And particularly inexplicable would be the fact of experience that the judgment of conscience puts itself not seldom in direct opposition to the practice and tenets of society; that for the sake of the higher ideal right, it denies and combats the right that exists, as we see in all the reformers and heroes of moral progress. An unprejudiced consideration of these different facts of experience will, as I believe, lead to the result that in the conscience there are two different factors bound up into unity—namely, an innate or *a priori* factor, and an *a posteriori* or empirical factor. On the innate element rests the always self-identical, abiding, formal character of the judgment of conscience, the unconditionedness with which it commands and judges; while upon the acquired element rests the manifoldness and changeableness, or the historical conditionedness, of its particular contents. Kant had well considered that first factor of the conscience, and had emphatically accentuated the fact that it is the demand of the reason which speaks to us so categorically. But Kant stopped halfway in referring the moral law to the subjective reason of the separate individuals, to their thought of the similar mode of acting of all, to this merely formal thinking without any essential determination of purpose; and as he also again identified this lawgiving reason with the freedom of individuals, there resulted the strange thought that the freedom of each individual gives itself the law to which he and all others owe obedience.

But how can a law which the freedom of every one makes, be binding upon the freedom of all? Nay more, how can it be unconditionally obligatory even for the freedom of the subject himself who has made it? Will it not be capable of being denied and annulled at any time by the same freedom from which it is thought to have sprung? In truth the matter stands, after all, quite otherwise: we find the moral law as a norm which is in nowise produced by our freedom, but which is rather presupposed by it, and is super-ordinated to it; and to this norm we feel ourselves bound—we owe obedience to it whether we will or not. An authority demanding obedience like this, to which each individual as well as others knows himself bound to subordinate himself, cannot possibly spring out of the freedom of the individual person, just as little as it can out of the compulsion of society which could only produce a compulsive "must" but not the moral obligation of the conscience. We shall accordingly recognise in the conscience the manifestation of the universal rational will which forms the better self, the essential nature of man in accordance with the divine image, which binds the individual to a purposive order of the universe, a kingdom of good or of God, and which is therefore rightly called a revelation of the holy will of God.

But in seeing in the conscience, on the side of its *a priori* factor, the subjective revelation of the divine will, we do not mean thereby to exclude in any way the psychological mediation and historical conditionedness of the judgments of conscience. As the laws of our thinking, which are originally inherent in our theoretical mind, can only exert and develop themselves on the material of knowledge that is presented by the world, and thus rise to our consciousness, so is it also with the norm of our moral judgments of value, which is originally inherent in our practical reason; it develops itself and comes into our consciousness only in reciprocal intercourse with society. The forms of the social order of life which arise in the course of human coexistence, and which correspond to the purposes of human community, awaken in the individual, as he grows up in the midst of them, the innate rational impulse which aims at the establishment of an inner order, at the harmonising of the manifold impulses and motives of our nature. This inner rational impulse corresponds to the external order of society with sympathetic receptivity; it finds in that order spirit of its spirit, and recognises it therefore as a justified authority. But as the inner moral capacity then develops and strengthens itself under the education of the external authority, the matured personality comes to such independence in its moral judgment that it begins to test even the social authorities and observances founded thereon as to how far they correspond to the absolute authority, or to what is rational and good in itself. Only in so far as the right that exists in society stands in harmony with the idea of right that presses itself internally upon such an individual does he recognise that right as an unconditionally binding authority—a distinct proof of the fact that this recognition has its proper basis, not in external facts, not in the brutal violence of the power that gives itself out for right, but in the idea of right that unconditionally binds the conscience, of which idea all positive right is always only an imperfect and perfectible expression. In this *Idea of Right* the religious consciousness recognises the revelation of the holy will of God; and this Idea creates an organism for itself in the external right of the social order, in which organism, although it is never perfectly realised, but is always striving to realise itself more perfectly, the religious consciousness recognises the revelation of the righteousness of God.

The religious conviction that the divine righteousness rules over human fates, appears to be opposed by the experience that right often succumbs and that wrong triumphs, that the just man suffers and perishes, while the godless man enjoys an undisturbed prosperity. It is from these experiences that have arisen those doubts of the righteousness of the government of the world which we find not merely among the heathen, but which have likewise received touching expression at the hands of many of the Biblical writers (as in Psalms, Ecclesiastes, and Job). But belief always again rescued itself from these mysteries of the actual world through the hope of future adjustment; it *demanded* that the proof of the retributive justice which appeared to be missing in our present experience must show itself in some sort of adjustment and establishment of the right order in this world or the next. From this resulted the so-called proof for God's existence drawn from the idea of retribution. Kant appropriated it in his well-known postulate that there must be a God who guarantees the establishment of the highest good in the combination of happiness with virtue. Thus apprehended, this "*Proof*" is naturally untenable, for objection is rightly raised against it by the question, What, then, gives us, from the standpoint of the rigoristic Kantian morals, the right to demand a rewarding of virtue by happiness? Besides, Hume had already reminded us that it is a very arbitrary conclusion to infer from the failing of the wished-for retribution in that sphere of reality which we alone know, its coming in a problematic future. Of course, viewed logically, this is quite inadmissible; but viewed psychologically, the judgment presents itself more favourably: for what else ultimately is the confident demand of a future retribution than just the childlike expression of the firm faith that right must still remain right, and show itself to be the victorious power over reality, whereas wrong must be confounded? This is the faith in the "Moral World-Order," which Fichte explained as the kernel of the Kantian postulate and put in the place of the belief in God, and which also the ethical idealists of the present day (such as Matthew Arnold) declare to be the kernel of religion in general.

We may certainly honour the moral value of this

faith, and yet doubt whether it is fitted to be a substitute for faith in God. To me it cannot but appear that the conception of the "Moral World-Order" suffers in most of those who hold it from an obscurity which is more or less concealed by rhetoric and a wavering between two very different things—namely, between the represented ideal of an order which ought to be, and the actual yet not ideal order in the world of experience. The latter order, as being a fact of experience, cannot be an object of faith; and besides, it suffers from so great defects that we can be little edified by its contemplation, but feel ourselves driven to rise above it to the Ideal. The Ideal, on the other hand, however perfect we may think it, always suffers from the one defect, that it is merely a representation of our subjective wishes and hopes, and is separated by a wide gulf from the world of the actual. Then the great question arises, How can the Ideal become actual and the actuality ideal? The solution of this decisive question appears to me to be hopeless so long as there is not known, besides the unreal Ideal and the unideal reality, a third thing in which the synthesis of the two sides would be guaranteed. For if the "Moral World-Order" were only the subjective thought of myself and of certain other men, it would be impossible to see what would ever entitle us to expect its realisation in the objective world. Such a thought would then have no more significance than any pious wish or beautiful dream. All the poetry which we might lay into this dream could not deceive us for a moment regarding the total groundlessness of our hope of its realisation. That thereby the religious faith would dissolve itself into an æsthetic play with unreal illusions is clear. If we would guard ourselves against this, it appears to me that the only view remaining is that our thought of the "Moral World-Order" is not merely *our* human Ideal, but the divine idea of the Good, revealing itself in our moral consciousness on the one side, and in the historical process of the development of human civilisation on the other; and that it therefore is a purposive thought of the Infinite Spirit, who is at once the Almighty Ground and the Eternal Law of the development of the world in time. Then, but also only then, have we a rational ground for the belief that the world is constituted for the realisation of the good; that the good, because it is one with the almighty will of God, is the power which will conquer the world in infinite progress, as it has already hitherto conquered it in part. When we thus look with the eye of the faith which is based on God into the historical world, we also find infallibly in it, notwithstanding all its evils and painful disharmonies in detail, the traces of the ruling of that governing righteousness and wisdom, which so directs the course of things that, in spite of all the wrong in individual things, right nevertheless comes in the whole of humanity to an ever firmer and purer existence. All the resistance which the realisation of the good finds everywhere in detail cannot hinder us from recognising its victorious progress in the whole of the world's history; and the very fact that it constantly asserts itself only in conflict with the resisting will of individuals—nay more, that their very resistance contributes as a spur and stimulus to the ever richer and more powerful development of the moral idea—enables us to recognise the more distinctly the revelation of the divine will as the ground and law of the moral process of humanity. There lies a deep truth in the words of the apostle, "For God hath concluded them all in disobedience, that He might have mercy upon all." The holy righteousness of God does not exert itself in order that it may keep men in the unfree innocence of childhood, and prevent any disunion of their will with the good; but it celebrates its highest triumph in this, that it reconciles those who are so disunited, and transforms sinners into saints.

We have thus already come upon the revelation of God in *Religion*. That it is customary to limit the conception of "Revelation" to Religion, or at least to refer that conception to it in quite a special sense, has so far a good reason in its favour, seeing that here more than anywhere else God enters into the human consciousness immediately as God—*i.e.*, as the one foundation and concluding goal of the whole World-Order and of the whole life of man,—as the Eternal One who, as it were, unveils Himself to the finite Spirit face to face. But the opinion held that on that account the religious revelation is absolutely different from all other revelation, and that as purely "supernatural" it stands out of comparison with—nay, even in opposition to—all revelation in the natural and moral order of the world, is an error of dogmatic reflection which cannot be maintained before an unprejudiced view of religious history. Religious revelation is also an *ordered* revelation, mediated both by the religious self-consciousness and by the religious fellowship. In the latter the individual finds the accumulated sum of religious experiences, which constitutes the common consciousness of a community, and which find expression in their forms of belief and worship. Through the communication and appropriation of this religious common consciousness, the individual religious life is awakened and formed, just as the individual moral life is by the social moralisation, and as the theoretical life is by the universal fund of knowledge and culture in the surrounding circle. But this capability of cultivation on the part of the individual presupposes a corresponding spiritual capacity, the rational impulse innate in the man, which as theoretical strives towards the ordering of his representations under the idea of Truth, as practical towards the ordering of the impulses of his will under the idea of the Good, and as religious towards a supreme unity of all that is true and good under the idea of God. The "religious impulse" is therefore an exercise of the same universal rational capacity which lies at the basis of science and morality; but it is the potentiated closing exercise of that capacity, for it tends not merely towards the ordering of the one or other side of consciousness, but towards the harmonious ordering of the *whole* personal life, under the highest regulative idea, the subjective correlate of the absolute principle of the universe. But we only become conscious of this innate religious capacity within us, as in the case of the theoretical and moral capacities, by the fact that it actually develops itself; and, moreover, it can only develop itself in reciprocal intercourse with the religious community, of which the individual is a member. This coexistence and separate existence of the two sides, of the individual religious subject and of the historical community, constitutes the "Religious World-Order," which is the highest stage of the order of the world, and the one in which the revelation of God completes itself in the most spiritual form. The religious revelation is therefore to be sought neither merely in the pious soul of the individual, who indeed only obtains his definite content in reciprocal intercourse with his community; nor is it merely to be obtained in the historical life of the religious community, which indeed only contains the sum of the religious experiences which have been handed down through many generations by the intercourse of the individuals with each other. The objective religion of the historical community is a product of the historical development of the religious capacity of its individuals, and is at all times capable and needful of further development through new contributions of the individuals. It is just in this advancing development of the religious capacities of our race, under the reciprocal furtherance of the individuals through the community and of the community through the individuals, that the ordered course of religious revelation consists. And it shows itself therein to be as conformable to law as the revelation in the natural and moral order of the world. If we turn our attention especially to those epochs and phenomena of the history of religion to which the conception "Revelation" is wont to be applied in a pre-eminent sense, we perceive everywhere, within as well as without the Biblical religion, the same relation of inner and outer, personal and social, traditional and new, as that belongs generally to the order of the historical life.

It is a defect of the present realistic theory of development that it underestimates or entirely overlooks the significance of *personality* in history, and endeavours to find the active forces of progress only in the masses. The masses, however, are never spiritually creative. All new world-moving ideas and ideals have proceeded from individual personalities, and even they have not arbitrarily devised them or found them out by laborious reflection, as men find out scientific doctrines by investigation; but they have received them by that involuntary intuition, which is also participated in by the artistic genius, and which everywhere forms the privilege of original genius, to whose eye the essence of things and the destination of men are disclosed. But certain as it is that every revelation is primarily a personal living experience, received and formed in the depths of the individual genius, yet in the thousand-fold echo which its communication awakens in others, there is always betrayed the fact that there has only come to right expression in it what had already slumbered unconsciously or lay darkly divined in the souls of others. Not that on that account the revelation is to be considered as a product of the common consciousness of its time—that is, of the opinions of the majority just then dominant. To these opinions the prophet of higher truth stands at all times rather in a polemical relation, as shown by innumerable examples in history, from the time of the Old Testament prophets down to the present day. Yet in all such cases the revelation of the religious genius is the expression of what the best men of their time have divined and longed for, the unveiling of their own better self, the fulfilment of their own highest hopes. It is just upon this that the power of a revelation proceeding from an individual to form a community, rests. While the prophet testifies by word and deed of the divine truth which has become revealed to him, and which dominates his whole personal life, he works through the collective impression of his personality attractively upon others, awakens in them the same spiritual experiences, inspires them for the same ideals, and thus founds a common higher life, a community of believers in which the revelation of the one becomes the common consciousness of the many. In this very power to awaken faith, to produce a common spiritual life in many, lies the self-proof which the revelation needs for its truth wherever it appears. Along with this "Proof of the Spirit and of Power" which he who is seized by it immediately experiences in his believing surrender to it, any other proofs from external "Signs and Wonders" are superfluous and useless; for as all revelation is originally an *inner* living experience—the springing up of religious truth in the heart—no external event can belong in itself to revelation, no matter whether it be naturally or supernaturally brought about. At most it may be an accompanying sign of such revelation by which the authority of the prophet is attested. But even the attestation of the person of the prophet is effected much more surely by the collective impression, and the effect of his appearance upon the world of his time and after-ages, than by extraordinary single miracles which he may have performed. In the case of these miracles it always remains very difficult, even for his contemporaries, and still more so for those who live in later times, to distinguish what actually happened from the embellishment of the narrators and the additions of legends; and then the interpretation of what happened must still remain so problematical that a firm conviction of religious truth is not capable of being founded upon it. Let us not forget that even Jesus Christ was so far from binding religious belief to external signs, that He rather reproves those for their unbelief who sought after such signs; and He referred them instead of this to the "signs of the time"—*i.e.*, to the prognostications and warnings which the historical situation of the present contains for the intelligent mind.

That the religious revelation is a historically ordered revelation is shown further by this, that it never appears unprepared or abruptly, but always "when the fulness of the time has come"—that is to say, when the inner and outer religious and social conditions of its possibility are given, when the average common consciousness is so far matured that it is able to apprehend the new ideas, when the external state of society is favourable to a spiritual crisis and movement, and especially when the need of the time increases the longing of the heart for higher truth. Then the new appears as the "fulfilment" of the old, in the negative and positive sense, abolishing what was untrue in it, and preserving and clarifying what in it was true. It is a regularly recurring characteristic of all religious heroes, reformers, and founders of religion, that they never wish merely to bring in a new thing; but with their opposition to the immediate actuality of the present, they yet always appear to attach themselves to the old, and even to set before themselves openly as their end the restoration of the purer faith of the fathers. Thus the prophets of Israel appealed to the fathers of Israel, Jesus appealed to the prophets, and Luther to apostles and prophets. Yet in all such cases the attachment to the old was not simply mere restoration of it, for in history there are no simple repetitions. Old truths are put by their application to new relations in time, under new points of view; they are brought into new combinations; certain sides which were formerly important retreat into the background, new positions become central, and new consequences are drawn. Thus out of the old there actually always arises a new thing which now corresponds to the wants of its present time, in the same way as the old had corresponded to the earlier stage of human development. The continuity and conformity to law of the development, as distinguished from a radical revolution, consists in this, that there is not simply a mere breach made with the traditional, but that the valuable product of the past is received and made a constituent part of higher truth, and is therefore preserved and at the same time developed, while that which in the old had significance *only* for its time is set aside, whether it be by direct conflict or by silent repulsion. This is the immanent *criticism* which carries on its function in all living development, and not less in the development of the religious revelation. That in this sphere the criticism which history itself in its progress performs on the old is recognised with more difficulty than in other spheres, and is indeed very often entirely denied, is easily explained from the conservatism of the religious consciousness, which fears for the security of its faith, if it were to admit the humanly imperfect even in the history of revelation and the capability of a higher perfection in every form of development in time. And yet it ought not to be difficult to perceive that we men are never able to possess the treasure of divine truth otherwise than in the earthen vessels of our limited forms of consciousness, which are obscured by many an error and prejudice. Dr James Martineau says excellently on this subject: " Whatever higher inspiration visits our world must use our nature as its organ, must take the mould of our respective capacity and mingle with the existing life of thought and affection. How then can it both assume their form and escape their limitation? how flow into the currents of our minds without being diluted there?"[1]

However high a religious hero may tower above his time, yet he is always in many respects a child of his

[1] Seat of Authority in Religion, p. 289.

age, prepossessed by its ideas and expectations. Nay more, he can only work upon his age by the fact that he has his spiritual roots in it, and consequently also still has a certain share of its limitations; and hence the new, which he reveals, can always pass only relatively beyond the old, and only gradually loosen itself entirely from its bonds. Revelation in unveiling new truths always sets new tasks for the advancing knowledge of its believers. Thus Christ Himself says in the Gospel of John : " I have yet many things to say unto you, but ye cannot bear them now. Howbeit, when He, the Spirit of truth, is come, He will guide you into all truth." And the apostle, who had recognised the " new " of Christianity in its relation to Judaism more acutely than all the others, yet also confesses of himself: " For now we see through a glass darkly ; now I know in part." "Not as if I had already attained, either were already perfect; but I follow after, if that I may apprehend."

The historical order of the religious revelation, that it is a development from lower to ever higher stages, a development in which the new is always at once the fulfilment and the criticism of the old, becomes nowhere more clearly apparent than in the relation of Christianity to Judaism. "Think not that I am come to destroy the law, or the prophets ; I am not come to destroy, but to fulfil." This expression, which stands solemnly at the culminating-point of the Sermon on the Mount, has been authoritative for the Christian Church at all times. It decidedly rejected from the beginning the opinion of Marcion, that the Christian God is another than the God of the Old Testament, as a heresy; and it has recognised in the law of Moses and in the prophets the revelation of the one true God, who "at sundry times, and in divers manners, spake in time past unto the fathers by the prophets," and who has "in these last days spoken unto us by His Son" (Heb. i. 1, 2). And in fact, if a religious revelation is to be found anywhere, it is certainly to be found in the spirit of the Hebrew prophets, who knew that God is the will of the morally good. This knowledge, which is of infinite reach and range, arose among them many centuries before Plato, and they grasped this truth still more purely than that profound thinker. For while in Plato the morally good, in the genuine Greek way, still blends in one with the beautiful, and is therefore not yet recognised in its full purity as the sublime ideal in its deep opposition to natural existence; in the Hebrew prophets, on the other hand, God is the holy will of the good, who, infinitely exalted above human weakness, makes His absolutely perfect purpose to men the law of their life, and lays claim to unconditional obedience. And in the light of this moral ideal they have not merely judged the life of individuals, but have also interpreted the fates of their people and of the nations of the world generally. Heathenism has indeed a nature-religion and a nature-philosophy, but it has neither a religious view of history nor a philosophy of history; for it knew no absolute final moral purpose to the attainment of which the fates of the nations were to serve as means. Israel, on the other hand, knew such a purpose of history—namely, the realisation of a kingdom of God, of a human fellowship and community corresponding to the holy will of God. In the light of this ideal the present always appeared insufficient to the prophets, and consequently their look was constantly directed to the future. Their belief in God was at the same time the hope of a divine future for their people and for human society; it was the spur which prevented them from resting sated and satisfied with any given things, but gave their wills infinite energy to combat the opposition of the present to their idea, and to keep their gaze fixed on the ideal time of salvation as the goal of their longing, striving, combating, and enduring. Thus did they become the path-finders and leaders of our race upon its toilsome way to the moral ideal of humanity. And because they recognised this goal as the purpose of God, they found everywhere in the living events of history the ruling of a purposive righteousness and wisdom, which the course of nature, as well as the politics of the powers of the world, was compelled to subserve as a means in order to carry forward the eternal end to its fulfilment—that is to say, as a means for the chastisement, the purification, the education of the people of God, out of whom the kingdom of God was to come. Thus did they become —not for Israel alone, but for mankind—the teachers of the religious view of the world which contemplates all that is perishing, all that is transitory, *sub specie æternitatis;* which makes the brightening gleam of hope fall upon all that is dark in the present; and which supports man's power of enduring and combating, by fixing his gaze upon the infinite infallible victory of the divine cause, the good and the true.

And yet even the illumined gaze of these Old Testament men of God was still confined within the limits of their own people and of their own age. True as the thought was, that history is the means used by the divine righteousness for the realisation of the kingdom of God, yet the idea of this kingdom was still imperfect, because it was too narrowly limited to the particular people of Israel. And from this there resulted a sensible obscuration of the idea of God—as if God were only the God of the Jews and not also of the heathen, as if He had only benevolence for the former and malevolence for the latter;—an opinion which in the post-prophetic Judaism became that religious pride which we encounter in such a repugnant form in the Pharisees of the time of Jesus. In like manner the true thought that the will of God is the law of our life still suffers in Judaism from a sensible defect. While the will of God was identified with the sum of the individual dogmas which grew out of the priestly legislation in the course of centuries, and when the same unchangeable authority was assigned to all these, and their exact fulfilment was made the chief thing, there arose that external legality which put the truly pious disposition below the performance of religious observances, and turned religion into a legal relationship of performance and reward. In such a relation no inner unity of the human will with the divine will is reached, but man sees in God only the retributive Judge before whose punishment he trembles or to whose reward he lays claim. Slavish fear and self-righteous reckoning with God are the unlovely features of this Jewish religion of law, to which the ethical idealism of the prophets had degenerated, and these traits strike us most visibly in Pharisaism.

It was *this* side of the Old Testament religion to which Christianity took a critical and destroying attitude, while it revealed a new and higher knowledge of God. "For," says Paul, "ye have not received the spirit of bondage again to fear; but ye have received the Spirit of adoption, whereby we cry, Abba, Father." In the pure soul of Jesus the God of the prophets and Psalms had become revealed as the merciful Father who maketh His sun to rise on the just and the unjust, and whose sons we are all to become, by becoming like Him in merciful brotherly love. It is true that even here the will of God is, and continues to be, the holy law, with whose fulfilment or non-fulfilment life or death for every one is connected; but the content of the divine will is no longer formed by a sum of external dogmas, but is comprehended in the one great commandment, "Love the Lord thy God with all thy heart, and thy neighbour as thyself." God's requirement in the new covenant to man is not less but greater than in Judaism; for He requires nothing less than the surrender of the whole undivided heart to His will. But the will of God has as its end nothing but the good—that is, man's becoming perfect in likeness to God, in which his true good, his eternal salvation, is also contained. Thus the good is here no longer a hard obligation which constantly excites the self-will only to rebel against it; but it is the Ideal in which man recognises the requirement of his own true being, to which he therefore surrenders himself, not in blind obedience, but in free and trusting love, certain of this, that in the surrender of himself to the divine purpose of the universal Good—to God's kingdom—he does not lose his soul, but preserves it; that it is only in unity with God that he becomes truly man, and free and happy. When man gets this experience of the liberating and blessing power of goodness, of love, and of faith, in himself and others, he recognises therein the working of the divine spirit. He recognises, therefore, that God does not as the holy lawgiver only *command* the good, but that as the holy spirit of love and inspiration he *creates* and effectuates the good itself (as Augustine said, "*Jube quod vis et da quod jubes*"). But then God is the good not merely in the sense of a sublime far-off Ideal, which stands in judgment over against the weak existence of men; but this Ideal is at the same time an ever active reality; it is the power to realise itself in the hearts of men and in the historical life of mankind; it is the power of the world, the truth of Being in general.

If we now look back from this height of the Christian knowledge of God to the development of the consciousness of God in the history of religion, it can hardly escape us that that high point was the goal to which the whole development strove from the beginning, and which is already prefigured in the religious capacity of man. For in some form or other these two things are always contained together in the belief in God: an Ideal of what ought to be, and that this is, at the same time, the power and the ground of real being. That God is the Ideal of moral goodness, that He is the Holy Will, was the revelation of Israel. But that this will of Goodness is the love which communicates itself to us, and which has constituted and guided nature and history, in order to realise itself in humanity as a kingdom of love—this is the revelation of Christianity, in which all the religious presentiment and longing of humanity before Christ comes to its fulfilment. Now, as the end of a development must also always be thought of as its ground and law, we shall now be entitled to say that the love which was recognised at the culminating-point of the history of religion as the essence of God, was even from the very beginning the ground of the human consciousness of God, which indeed could only disclose itself gradually to the consciousness of men, in the slow march of the human development, as the content of their belief in God. This is the sense in which we use the term when we designate the revelation of God in the religious Order of the World as revelation of His *love*.

"Thou hast created us for Thyself, and our heart is restless till it has come to rest in Thee." This beautiful expression of Augustine is in fact the key to the whole history of religion. In the universal experience that man's nature is so constituted that some kind of consciousness of God is inevitable to him, although it may be only a presentiment or a search, we must recognise the original revelation of the love of God. All human consciousness of God presupposes a self-communication of God, a working of the divine Logos in the finite spirit. Now as the consciousness of God is a constitutive element of the human species, it may be rightly said that the whole of humanity is the object of the divine love, that it is an Immanuel and son of

God, that its whole history is a continual incarnation of God—as indeed it is also said in Scripture that we are a divine offspring, and that we live and move and have our being in God. But what lies potentially *in* the human consciousness of God, is not on that account also manifestly revealed *to* it from the beginning. If the heathen peoples generally attributed benevolent sentiments to their particular protecting deities, yet they were far from knowing the essential nature of the Deity, as such, to be Love; rather did the course of nature, with its incalculable vicissitudes and constantly threatening dangers, appear to them to point to a malevolent, capricious and envious, jealous and malicious disposition in the divine powers that rule in nature. In Herodotus the envy of the Deity still plays a prominent part in human history. It was Plato who first rejected this opinion, and recognised unenvious goodness as the essential nature of the Deity. But this purer belief in God did not become popular; the enlightenment of Epicureanism put chance in the place of the divine government, and held the gods to be indifferent spectators of human fates, while the superstitious dread of evil demons increased among the multitude with the pessimistic mood of the time. In the prophets of Israel there are found glorious expressions concerning the love of Jahve to His elect people; but beside this love stands the hate of Jahve against the enemies of Israel. "Jacob have I loved, and Esau have I hated." In the Psalms the religious relationship is individualised; the feeling of the pious man rises often to such an intimate familiarity with the merciful and gracious God, that it comes home to us like a Christianity before Christ. But the increasing legal character of the Jewish religion brought along with it the consequence that the fundamental view of God was that of the just judge, and that it left no room for love. In addition to this came the fact that so long as the manifestation of the divine benevolence was sought pre-eminently in external happiness, the experience of the misfortune of the just always awakened those doubts of the goodness of God of which the Book of Job and Ecclesiastes bear witness. The idea of God in Judaism had not yet advanced to a pure spiritual morality, and therefore could neither free itself from the limits of the popular view, nor even exhibit itself in contrast to the evil of the world and the sin of man as the overcoming and redeeming power. It was the Christian faith in God that first rose to the pure ethical idealism which knows God absolutely as spirit and love, as the unconditioned will of the good which is neither bound to national limits nor withdraws powerlessly before the sin of men, but which rather reveals its victorious power most wonderfully to the world of sinners itself,—not as punishing justice, but as redeeming grace which makes all new and good, which transforms sinners into children of God and unites the divided humanity into a kingdom, nay, into a family of God, a fellowship of brethren who are animated by *one* spirit, the holy spirit of love.

As certain as it is that the highest revelation of God is first to be found in this faith, it would as certainly be a great error if we were to separate this high stage of revelation from the other stages of it, or even to put it in opposition to the revelation in the moral order of the world. This error appeared in a peculiarly striking form among those heretics of the second century who opposed the good God of the Gospel to the just but not good God of the old covenant—heretics whom the Church decidedly repudiated from the beginning. But the same error is committed very frequently in a finer form even *within* the Church, wherever divine grace is represented as an arbitrary sympathy of God with some at the cost of others, and of the righteousness of God, as if God were to suppress His righteousness in certain cases and make grace take the place of right in some individuals. This is a crude anthropomorphism which has brought much confusion into the Christian idea of God. The divine love, even as forgiving grace, is always one with His holy righteousness; for it is one and the same Will of goodness which in its self-communication to sinful men immovably asserts its holy purpose, in releasing man from his sin and transforming him into a new man, who "lives in the spirit" and is thereby freed from the guilt and damnableness of sin. The forgiveness of sin is everywhere one with the subdual of it. The inviolability of the moral order of the world is therefore not annulled even by the Christian order of salvation. It only ceases to be a judging power against man, seeing that it has itself become the living power of love in him, which voluntarily subordinates itself as a subservient member, to the purpose of the whole. Grace can therefore only come into operation where the moral conditions are present for its reception, and these moral conditions cohere with the universal state of the moral development, as it is brought about in the life of society, under the co-operation of the manifold educative factors. The working of grace is therefore as little an arbitrary working as is that of Omnipotence. As the latter is regulated by the laws of the natural world, so is the former by the laws of the moral world; as the divine Omnipotence reveals itself, not in the annulment or interruption of the order of nature, but in the purposeful constitution and preservation of nature as a means for the spiritual and moral life, even so the love of God reveals itself, not in the annulment of the moral order of the world, but in the purposeful government of history, through which it becomes the education and training for the highest end of the kingdom of God.

If we now finally reflect upon the oneness of the whole order of the world, how it exhibits one purposively guided development from the lowest stages of existence up to the highest perfection of the spiritual life in the fellowship of love and faith — in this we cannot but perceive the revelation of the divine *wisdom*. The question might indeed be raised why that wisdom is here spoken of for the first time, seeing that Nature already bears evidence of the wisdom of the Creator through its purposiveness and beauty? Certainly it is so; but on the other hand we must not forget that final ends are nowhere to be recognised within nature, but that it presents an endless change of becoming and perishing, of the furtherance of life and the checking and annihilation of life, so that looking only at nature we may often rather receive the impression of a purposeless play than of a wisdom pursuing definite designs. Even human life, viewed only from the natural standpoint, is no exception to this universal condition of the life of nature. Nature has not surrounded the life of man with greater care than that of other living beings. He has to undergo the same struggle for existence amid the thousandfold dangers and needs of his life; and he feels his evils even more keenly, because more conscious than other beings. But what follows from these facts? Surely only what is already otherwise certain to the pious consciousness— namely, that the final end of the government of the world is not to be primarily sought in the natural life, but in the spiritual and moral life. But even in that life it is not the changing fates of individuals, peoples, and kingdoms, in which we can yet find the highest and lasting final end of history. Even these show themselves, through the course of thousands of years, again and again as mere ministering means and fore-stages for the realisation of the one universal kingdom of God, which is destined to unite all men as children of God in brotherly love. Only in such a universal fellowship, in which the individuals are bound together through the same devotion of all to the common end of humanity—to the Ideal of the good and true—can we behold the ultimate final end of history. Certainly this is an Ideal from which the actuality appears to be infinitely far removed. But is it a mere abstract idea to which nothing in the actual world corresponds? I think assuredly that with the entrance of Christianity into the world, the firm foundation for its realisation has been laid, so that the whole history of the world prior to Christianity may be regarded as the preparation for the realisation of that Ideal, and the whole of Christian history as the development of it. If, therefore, the whole history of the world shows itself as the teleological process of the advancing realisation of the divine purpose of the world, we are entitled to find in the history of the world the revelation of the world-governing wisdom of God. But do not the fates of the various peoples, tribes, families, individuals, also belong to the whole of the world's history? If, therefore, the wisdom of God is manifestly revealed in the whole, shall we not then also be able to confide in its wondrous guidance, where much remains dark and mysterious in detail regarding the fates of peoples and men? The more we look away from what is individual and small to the great and whole, the more we free ourselves from particular egoistic purposes and seek first after the kingdom of God: in short, the wiser we ourselves become in our thinking and acting, so much the more shall we admire the wisdom of God in the order of the world, and say with the Apostle, "O the depth of the riches both of the wisdom and knowledge of God! How unsearchable are His judgments, and His ways past finding out. . . . For of Him, and through Him, and to Him, are all things: to whom be glory for ever. Amen."

LECTURE VII.

THE RELIGIOUS VIEW OF MAN.

I. HIS ESSENTIAL NATURE AND HIS ACTUALITY.

"LORD, what is man, that Thou art mindful of him? and the son of man, that Thou visitest him?" This utterance of the Psalmist is a classical expression of the two aspects which we always meet beside each other in the religious contemplation of man—namely, his lowliness, powerlessness, and need of help, in contrast to the divine loftiness; and again, on the other hand, his highness and dignity in contrast to the other creatures, his affinity with God and his being made in conformity with the image of God. The latter side we find expressed in most religions under different legendary forms. To it belong, in the first place, the many legends of the divine descent of men, whether it be of all men or at least the primeval ancestors of a particular people, or even of individual prominent persons, heroes, kings, and wise men, of prehistoric times. To it further belong the legends of the creation of men by special divine contrivance. For example, according to the Biblical legend, God, with His own hands, formed the body of Adam out of earth and breathed into him the breath of life, so that man thus appears as a mixed product of earthly matter and divine spirit. In the later legend of the creation in the Bible, contained in Genesis i., God created man after His own image and likeness as the close and crown of the whole work of creation, with the destination to rule over the earth and animals. By the "Image of God" is here meant the whole superiority of man over the sub-human creation, his higher bodily and spiritual equipment, which makes him capable of lordship over the earth.

The same thought of the distinguishing dignity of man is further expressed in the legends of an initial ideal state, a "Golden Age" of innocence and happiness, from which men sank by their own guilt into their present sorrowful condition. Well known is the legend in Hesiod of the Golden Age under the lordship of Kronos, when the happy human race lived free from cares and toils, in untroubled youth and cheerfulness, with a superabundance of the gifts which the earth furnished of herself: the race was indeed not immortal, but it experienced death even as a soft sleep. After the dying out of this happy race, then followed the Ages which became worse and worse: the Silver Age, the Brazen Age, and the Iron Age, each always more imperfect than the preceding one, both in moral worth and in natural wellbeing. In the legend of Prometheus, Epimetheus, and Pandora, the transition out of the state of nature into civilisation appears on the one hand as an achievement of the striving spirit of man, which knows how to procure for itself the heavenly gift of fire. But on the other hand, it also appears as an act of godless insolence, which the titanic man Prometheus must atone for by torturing bonds, till, becoming conscious of the impotence of his defiance, he is released out of his distress by the merciful help of the divine man Heracles, and is reconciled with the heavenly ones; while human weakness and wantonness—represented in Epimetheus—are punished by the box of Pandora out of which proceed all the evils and diseases which had been as yet unknown to the simple life of nature. According to the Persian legend, likewise, the first human pair was a good creation of the all-wise Spirit, Ahura, who had breathed into them his own breath. But soon the primeval men allowed themselves to be seduced by the hostile spirit Angromainyu into lying and idolatry, whereby the evil spirits obtained power over them and the earth, and spoiled the good creation. According to the Hebrew legend, which seems to have close relations with the Babylonian, the first parents found themselves at the beginning in the Garden of Eden under happy relationships, at peace with God and nature, and in childish innocence not ashamed of their nakedness. But when they transgressed the prohibition not to eat of the tree of knowledge, then they indeed really became knowing, for they began to be ashamed of their nakedness; but they had to atone for this progress in culture by the loss of the happiness of Paradise, in place of which came labour, pain, and death. Then, indeed, they made many useful and artistic inventions, but with every further step in civilisation they always removed further from God. Thus, according to this narrative too, a happy state of childlike innocence and naturalness forms the beginning; it is lost by man's own guilt, and in its place comes the career of culture with its titanic striving after equality with God and with manifold miseries, distress, and death. Wellhausen has strikingly summed up the common ground-thought of all these legends in the proposition, "It is the yearning-song which goes through all the peoples: having attained to historical civilisation, they feel the worth of the goods which they have sacrificed for it." Already the later Jewish theology, and still more the Christian theology since Augustine, interpreted the sense of the narrative of Genesis iii., contrary to the original meaning of its words, as signifying that the primeval state was not merely a state of childish innocence, but a state of moral and religious perfection, wisdom, and holiness; and that there was brought in by the Fall, not merely the external evils of life, but a complete perversion of human nature, with loss of the divine image, and all freedom for good, and the dominion of evil lust and of demons.

To the scientific view, it is self-evident that all such legends of an ideal state of humanity at the beginning are devoid of claim to any historical value. They contradict too palpably the fundamental law of all human history, that mankind must gradually win all truth and goodness through hard labour and constant struggle with rude nature. According to all that the science of antiquity has enabled us to know or to conjecture concerning the circumstances of the oldest prehistoric period, we must think of the primeval men, the further we go back, as engaged in an ever harder struggle for existence, as slowly overcoming nature by toilsome labour, and as only gradually struggling out of the rudest conditions of life into an elementary civilisation. The Golden Age of the beginning is therefore, as certainly as the "millennial kingdom" of the end, an *ideal image* in which the pious poetry of different peoples has deposited the wishes and hopes in which they sought to raise themselves above the wants of their actual life. But it is just in this that the high significance of all these legends consists. They testify that it is essential to humanity to form Ideals, and to hold them up before the reality as its antitype and the goal of its striving.

In the capability of and the impulse to the formation of Ideals we may discern the distinguishing essential mark of man. The beast follows the unchangeable instincts of his nature, which uniformly shape his life in every generation. It has no history, no progress, because it is not able to form Ideals beyond its actual condition at any time. Man, on the contrary, has a history, a development mounting upwards, because he is not satisfied with any given state as ultimate and definitive; but in his thinking he sketches the image of a better and ever better state, and this drives him restlessly on to strive higher and higher from one goal to another. This capability of forming Ideals rests primarily upon the capability of thinking as such — *i.e.*, of abstracting from the individual given representations, and combining them by the free activity of the synthetic imagination; and further, upon the impulse of reason to bring the manifold contents of consciousness into a single form corresponding to the unity of the self, to order the representations, feelings, and desires according to a norm lying in the thinking self, to shape the multiple and confused into the unity of a harmonious whole. This rational impulse towards the ordering of consciousness and life is endlessly active, because its goal can never be otherwise than relatively attained—that is, in an always only partial and ever unstable equilibrium of the psychological powers in relation with each other and with the external world. Hence every Ideal, every type sketched in thought of an order of life that ought to be, shows itself to be insufficient as soon as it is reached, and with this there is immediately given the necessity for the formation of a new and higher Ideal. In this infinite striving after something better than what is, is precisely exhibited man's destination for the unconditionally good, for his assimilation with the perfect Ideal, or God; and in this active destination *to* God is shown his descent *from* God, his being formed in the image of God, and his divine sonship. This, therefore, already dwells in man from the beginning, and forms his true nature as man; but it is not present in him from the beginning as an actual state of perfection, but only as a potentiality and impulse to become actually, through his own activity, that for which he bears in himself the divine capacity as a rational being. "Be ye perfect, as your Father in heaven is perfect." This is the infinite task of the human race, which it is not able to fulfil at any time otherwise than relatively and approximately, and from the fulfilment of which it was furthest removed at the beginning of its history.

If we ask now, In what does the Ideal of human perfection consist? only a formal definition can be given of it. For the real determination of that perfection becomes gradually more distinct to us only with the advancing development of human nature in history, and yet it can never be completely conceived, because the absolutely perfect transcends all experience. The Ideal of human perfection may perhaps be formally defined as the complete and harmonious realisation of all human capacities in a common life of humanity, such that in it all the several members (groups and individuals) are ends in themselves, and at the same time equally subservient members and instruments of the whole. That the Ideal is not to be thought of as merely individual but as universal, follows from this, that the reason which demands it is the same universal endowment in all—namely, the divine image in man; and that its actualisation in the individual would not be possible at all without its actualisation in the community, with which the individual is united by his social instincts in such solidarity that all disharmony in the formation of life in the community exerts a hindering influence also upon the harmonious formation of the life of the individual. But on the other hand, the Ideal is not to be thought merely as a social Ideal, as, for instance, a rational order of society, in which the individual persons would come into consideration only as means subservient to the whole, without the Ideal of man becoming actualised in and for his own life. In such a view it would be forgotten that reason is only active as an impulse in the consciousness of individual persons, and that its direct aim is by subordination of the sensuous to the spiritual impulses, and of the egoistic to the altruistic impulses, to establish in every personal life that harmonious order which we designate as morally good disposition or virtue. This can of course only happen through individuals living together with the community to whose ends they have subserviently to subordinate themselves. But the value of the objective ends of society is measured only by their furthering the personal life of all their members in the direction of the common Ideal of humanity. These two sides of the absolute Ideal of humanity—namely, the individual and universal—we find combined in the Christian idea of the "*kingdom of God,*" as the organised community of the children of God. Here the individual free personalities are filled and impelled by the divine spirit of goodness and truth; but even as such they are at the same time devoting themselves in love to the common end of the whole, to the will of God, which is over all and in all, and is binding them all to each other and making every one free in himself. Now, in so far as the kingdom of God is the universal realisation of the end of humanity, it forms the highest common good of all men; and participation in it, therefore, also includes the full self-satisfaction or happiness of every one. Personal happiness as a feeling of the inner harmony of life ought, indeed, not to be the final end of our moral striving—for that should only be God's kingdom and righteousness—but it is withal the accessory and the sign of faithful and successful labour for God's purpose, as Christ says: "Seek ye first the kingdom of God and His righteousness, and all other things shall be added unto you."

But this again raises the question, How can the absolute Ideal of the kingdom of God be the practical goal of our acting? How are we to derive from this universal idea definite directions for our individual conduct? Have there not been at all times much nearer and narrower ideas and goals to be striven after, by which men were determined in their thinking and acting? Undoubtedly; but let us not forget that all the limited ideals of human striving, in so far as men actually strove after rational ends, were and are nothing else but stations upon the infinite way to the actualisation of the absolute Ideal. This Ideal must necessarily resolve itself for the consciousness of men into the manifold relative Ideals which, partly along with each other and partly after each other, determine the living and striving of men. Side by side with each other we find the various Ideals of the individual peoples, always according to their natural endowment and place in the world. Again, in every people the moral collective will differentiates itself according to the individual classes and callings, according to families, and last of all even according to individuals. These coexisting moral goals stand to each other in a complementary relation like the parts of an organism. But changing Ideals also appear after one another like the changing phases in the development of the organic life. Every age has its peculiar Ideal, its special conception of the purpose of life, its estimation of the goods of life, and its particular labour at such a definite task of life as is demanded by the historical situation of its time. The more powerfully a definite Ideal of life rules the thinking and feeling of the whole community, so much the more does it stamp its special impress on the morals and laws, on the political and ecclesiastical institutions, and even on the art and science, of the age. It strives to embody itself in the common orders of life of the peoples, and to secure for itself lasting dominion. But this always succeeds only for a limited space of time. When an Ideal has attained to dominion, and has seemingly founded its authority firmly for all time in fixed institutions, the defects also forthwith make themselves visible which are connected with the dominion of every limited Ideal. Then a reaction arises in the mood of the peoples; critical reflection awakens; doubt of the absolute truth of the previous Ideal of life and of the orders of life that have sprung from it takes possession first of individuals, and then of ever greater masses of men, and in the conflict with the old there arises a new Ideal, the goal of the striving of coming generations. This in its turn again passes through the same circle of aspiring, conquering, and ruling, and of being combated and overcome. These transformations of human Ideals in the succession of ages form the true kernel of history, its spiritual substance, which all external events subserve as its means and expression.

Each of these changing Ideals is indeed for *its* time the ruling authority, which rightly lays claim to the devotion and labour of all; for it is the determinate form in which the absolute rational destination of humanity comes to consciousness on the stage of its development at the time, and in which it can and ought to actualise itself. But it is not yet on that account in itself the absolutely true and good, whose right would be universal and eternal; and where it gives itself out as this, its relative right becomes unright, its conditioned truth becomes untruth, which succumbs to the criticism of the mind that sees farther. On this rests the good right of all endeavours at reformation. But in this connection it is not to be overlooked that criticism of the relative Ideal of the time and of its embodiment in the existing orders of society is only justified in so far as it rests upon the knowledge of a higher Ideal, and in so far as it will and can serve to further the formation of the existing conditions into a better order. To such a critical reform it is always only the leading spirits, the gifted prophets of higher truth, who are called. They are the instruments of Providence in the education of humanity unto the absolute Ideal. For that reason their acting, although it puts itself in opposition to the authority of the existing conditions, is yet not arbitrary and immoral, but has the highest sanction of the divine will, which reveals itself in their conscience as a divine calling, before the unconditional obligation of which all other considerations, even those of the common duties of everyday life, give way. But how can this higher right, whose legitimation lies at first only in the breast of the prophet and reformer himself, be proved to *others?* The public " Proof of the Spirit and of Power" is effected only by history itself, which makes the deeds of the reformers the land-marks of new epochs of humanity. But before this can happen—at the beginning of the movement of reform—who will blame the common man if he can see in the bold innovators only violators of the holy order of right, of moral practice, and of faith, and if he fights for conscience' sake against what is yet in truth the cause of God?

What is most profoundly tragic in the world's history is that the divinely good and true can everywhere only introduce itself into reality by hard struggle, and that its most violent opponents are always, not the unideal egoists, but those who cling to the Ideals of the past and are not yet able to grasp those of the future. They have a zeal for God, but not of knowledge. If we would not become accomplices with them, we must be on our guard against the unideal moral positivism, which would find the good only in conformity to the order of society that exists at the time. We should never forget that all positive right, as well as all positive faith, is only relatively good and true, an expression for the time of the stage of development reached by the human mind, which is destined still to advance to higher goals. We shall then be able to find the criterion of the moral value of all acting only in its having for its motive the realisation of the absolute Ideal of humanity, through furtherance of its normal moral development and removal of the hindrances to it. In other words, the moral value of our acting consists in this, that it is conscious and willed co-operation with the divine purpose of history: the education of mankind into a kingdom of God, in which righteousness, peace, and joy in the Holy Ghost are to reign.

With the human capacity for the forming of Ideals, the capacity for the *bad* is inseparably connected. For the beast there is no badness, because its natural impulses and instincts are the laws of its life. But in the case of man, who has to order his desires by his reason, who as a thinking being sets ends to himself which are above immediate desire and independent of it, and who derives from the common ends common rules of acting according to which the social life of men is regulated, there is given the possibility of the disagreement of the self-will of individuals with the order of the whole,—in other words, we have here the possibility of badness. The bad, therefore, presupposes the idea of the good, or of what ought to be. To the man who is awakening to moral consciousness this always presents itself empirically at first in the form of moral practice and laws. Yet the idea of the good is not on that account identical with the objective moral practice of the society of the time, but has its deeper ground in the *a priori* demand of reason for a harmonious ordering of the active manifestations of the will, in each and in all. In the correlation of this internal endowment and those external facts of conscience and of practice consists the moral order of the world, in which we have already, in a former Lecture, recognised the revelation of the holy, just will of God. Accordingly the bad will have to be defined as the violation of the God-willed moral order of the world, by the self-will of individuals.

The opinion that badness is mere negation, want, and limit, has been often repeated from the time of Plato, and it has been especially represented by Spinoza; but it cannot be accepted as correct. As a matter of fact, physical badness is not mere want of power, for it rather consists in the disharmony of the powers and organs of life. In like manner, badness is not mere want of spiritual power, either of the will or of the understanding; for it is just in the worst forms of badness that uncommon energy of will and acuteness of understanding are often actually found. In opposition to the opinion of Socrates that badness rests upon ignorance, Aristotle already called the fact to mind that the doing of the good is not always combined with the knowing of it, seeing that it depends also on the passions. If badness consisted only in the want of knowledge, then those who are theoretically most cultivated must also be morally the best, which no one will venture to assert. And what, then, would be the meaning of the expression of the apostle Paul when he says, "The good that I would I do not: but the evil which I would not, that I do"? This self-contradiction between the actual ego and the better self, of the Ideal which is well known and recognised as the better which ought to be—this self-contradiction between rational will and self-will—is something quite different from mere not-knowing or deficient insight. Such a want of insight is found in the infant child, yet no one would judge its condition to be one of imputable guilt. Not less inappropriate is the frequent definition of badness as sensuousness; for the faculty of sense in itself is neither good nor bad, but, like all that is natural, indifferent. Any sensuous function only becomes bad when it appears in a moral being in disagreement with the moral order; and therefore it is just this violation of order that is bad, and not the sensuous faculty in itself.

What is correct in this view is only this, that among the manifestations of badness, allowing the unbridled sway of the sensuous impulses is one of the most frequent, but it is neither the only nor even the worst manifestation of badness. Vices like lying and hypocrisy, avarice, the lust of power, jealousy, cruelty, fanaticism, do not spring out of the sensuous nature, and just as little can they be referred to weakness of the spirit, seeing that they are often combined with extraordinary strength of understanding and will: they rest rather upon the dominion of the egoistic, and suppression of the altruistic impulses of our nature. This form of the bad is therefore worse than the sensuous, because it is more spiritual. The proper nature and the deepest principle of the bad unveils itself more immediately in this spiritual form than in the other sensuous forms—namely, as that self-wilfulness which seeks its own, unconcerned about the moral order or the ends and normal laws of the world as a whole.

The doctrine of the Church has explained the origin of badness from the Fall of our first parents in Paradise, and a brief state of perfect sinlessness was thought to have preceded the Fall. How little claim this ideal representation of the state of man at the beginning has to historical truth has been already remarked. But the further difficulty now presents itself, as to how, under the assumption of a perfectly sinless beginning, we are to conceive the possibility of the Fall? Badness could not arise out of a pure will of goodness, because no motives to it would exist, and without such no imputable action is thinkable. And this has been actually recognised by the Church Fathers, as they mostly sought to explain the Fall of our first parents from motives of pride, or unbelief, or concupiscence. But they have not considered that with the assumption of such motives they already admitted an internal existence of evil *before* the Fall, and thus the explanation of the origin of evil from the Fall breaks down. Nor is this difficulty diminished by the interpolation of an external tempter, whom (since the time of the "Wisdom of Solomon") it has been customary to think of as Satan, embodied in the serpent. But apart from the fact that thereby the first origin of the bad is thrust away from mankind back to the realm of spirits in the world beyond, where it becomes utterly inexplicable, the Fall would become not a whit more conceivable by following this circuitous route through the realm of demons. For all external incitements only become temptation by their letting loose an inner impulse to the bad, in the stirrings of which the real temptation first exists. As James truly says, "Every man is tempted when he is drawn away of his own lust, and enticed." Hence, even if we were willing to accept as a fact a temptation of our first parents by Satan, yet it must always again be regarded as having found a point of attachment in the inner bad lust and inclination of the first parents; and here we stand again before the same difficulty, without having obtained any help whatever from the hypothesis of a tempting Satan. The position accordingly will remain thus: that a first act of sin always already presupposes some inner condition of *being* sinful; and it therefore cannot be the first cause, but only the first manifestation, of sin.

But just as inconceivable as the Fall itself, would be also the consequences of it as they are described in the doctrine of the Church. No analogy of experience extends far enough to explain the corruption of the whole nature of the species in consequence of the single first deed of our first parents. Habitual tendencies of character do not proceed from individual actions, but only out of frequent repetitions of them. But that the free first use of freedom could have abolished this freedom itself, and thereby destroyed the moral capacity of man, is wholly unthinkable. Nor have the dogmatic theologians of the Church known how to help themselves out of the difficulty of this dilemma. Either the moral capacity and freedom (the Divine Image) belonged to the specific nature of man, and then it could not be lost; or it was lost, and then it could not belong to the specific nature, but was a mere accident of it (a *donum superadditum*, as the dogmatic theology of the Catholic Church teaches). The further assertion that contemporaneously with the moral nature of man his bodily nature was also corrupted by the Fall and made subject to death, presupposes that without the Fall the human body would have been immortal—an assumption which stands in manifest contradiction to all the laws of the order of nature. Besides, it may be recalled that according to the doctrine of the Bible throughout, perishableness belongs to the nature of all "flesh," and consequently also to the nature of the fleshly body of man. "Flesh and blood," says Paul, "cannot inherit the kingdom of God, nor can the corruptible put on incorruption;" yet he says nowhere that this condition did not come in till after the Fall, but he ascribes perishableness to the flesh generally as a property belonging to its essential nature. Again, the consequences of the Fall, which are inconceivable in a natural way, have been sought to be explained by a punitive miracle of the divine omnipotence. By this appeal to the supernatural the difficulties springing from natural experience would be indeed removed; but there arise immediately in their place almost even greater moral difficulties, such as, How are we to bring it into accordance with the divine justice, goodness, and wisdom, that He should have punished the first transgression of our first parents, who were still entirely inexperienced and untried, at once with the total corruption of the bodily and spiritual nature of the species, and consequently should have again annihilated His own work of creation? Nor can so singular an opinion appeal for its support to Holy Scripture. For when the apostle Paul says that "God hath concluded all in unbelief, that He may have mercy upon all," he cannot possibly have been of opinion that the sin of our first parents had been a traversing of the divine world-plan, or that it had brought about an alteration of the capacities originally implanted by the creation. Rather has Paul manifestly thought of the sin of man as included within the whole of the divine government of the world, and of the saving plan of redemption—namely, as the state of the natural humanity which necessarily precedes redemption and is to be removed by it, seeing that natural humanity could not, according to the eternal order of the world, be at first spiritual, or already so from the very beginning (1 Cor. xv. 46). Original perfection viewed as the state of man at the beginning is therefore as much a dogmatic fiction as is the consequent complete corruption. To the abstract ideal representation of the beginning corresponds the equally abstract caricature of the corruption following it. We shall rather have to think of the state of our first parents according to the analogy of the childlike innocence of all religions — that is, as a state in which good and bad, the impulses of the flesh and of the spirit, were already existent and active. But the consequences of the distinction of the two were then still wholly or almost wholly wanting—a state which is as far removed from moral perfection as from moral depravity, as it stands just upon the threshold of the passage from morally indifferent naturality to conscious morality.

Accordingly we cannot explain the origin of the bad from the Fall of our first parents, which cannot be established as a historical fact. But we can just as little give assent to that indifferentism according to which every man is viewed as wholly good by nature, and as having himself caused his becoming bad by an act of his own groundless arbitrary will. This view starts from the indifferentist conception of freedom, which rests upon a false abstraction. The real will is never an empty possibility as indeterminism presupposes, a possibility which can determine itself equally well on any side, and which after every action would be again equally empty and indetermined. Out of such indeterminateness a morally imputable acting could never proceed; for this presupposes conscious grounds of determination, and there can only be such for a will which has its determinate content in certain impulses and inclinations. Freedom is self-determination of the will, not in the sense of a determination out of groundless contingency, but self-determination on the ground of its own determined being, its temperament or character. As the man is, so he acts. The good tree brings forth good fruit, and the corrupt tree can bring forth only evil fruit. Undoubtedly all willing and doing react again upon the being who wills and does, improving or corrupting the condition of the character in some degree. The development of the moral life, as of all life generally, just consists in this, that "all is fruit and all is seed," that inner and outer enter into constant interaction with each other, and that all experience and acting enter as co-operating factors into the formation of character, out of which again the later acting proceeds as fruit. Only in this rests the possibility of a moral influencing of the will by education and instruction. Were every action a groundless arbitrary act of the indifferent will, it would be useless to impress upon man the best principles, as they would really give his character no determined direction, and consequently could never become permanent grounds for the determination of his acting. Then also no reliance upon any man would be possible; for any one, although he passed hitherto as the best of men, might the next moment by his groundless arbitrary will decide for the worst actions. But that the position is quite otherwise in reality we all know from daily experience. The more exactly we know men, the more certainly are we able also to calculate beforehand their mode of acting in the future. Whatever we may think theoretically regarding the freedom of the will, in the practical intercourse with men we always act and judge on the positive assumption that the individual actions of men are as certainly determined by their constant condition of will or sentiment, as the fruits of a tree are determined by its nature. In like manner we desire from the poet that he portray characters which develop their moral nature in a series of consistent actions; and the more he succeeds in this, so that all the individual external manifestations of a person coalesce into the whole of a unique and specifically determined character, so much the more does such poetic invention make upon us the æsthetically satisfying impression of the truth of life. Does there not lie in this an involuntary testimony to the fact that the theory of the *liberum arbitrium indifferentiæ* is an abstraction foreign to life and untrue?

We have seen that the explanation of the bad from the indifferent arbitrary will of individuals is untenable, on account of the psychological incorrectness of this conception. But it may be added that this mode of explanation also presupposes a superficial conception of the bad. Out of the freedom of the individual will there could continually proceed only individual bad actions, which through very frequent repetition might possibly also have bad inclinations as their consequence. But it is a very old experience, and one attested in manifold ways by the sacred Scriptures of almost all religions, that evil inclinations do not first arise out of free acting, but already precede it; nay more, that they have their roots in the deepest ground of human nature. "For the imagination of man's heart is evil from his youth." "Out of the heart proceed evil thoughts." "Every man is tempted when he is drawn away of his own lust, and enticed." These passages in the Bible are the expression of the same universal human experience which led Kant to the doctrine of the "radical badness" or of the perversity of the highest maxims of our will—an experience which cannot possibly be explained by reference to individual free acts of will, seeing that it rather precedes them; for earthly man when he awakes to moral consciousness always finds in himself already the propensity of a self-will that is contrary to law. If, however, this inclination were to be explained as arising out of the freedom of the individual, this could only be done by means of the predeterministic theory, which derives the origin of the bad from an intelligible act of freedom, presupposed as prior to the life in time. Plato had already in half-figurative allusions taught a fall of the souls pre-existing in the ideal world; and the Christian Church-father Origen had attached himself to it, without, however, finding approval on this point among the ecclesiastical theologians. In modern times the philosophers Kant, Schelling, and Schopenhauer have explained the bad from an intelligible act of freedom, and indeed from the same act, which (according to Schelling and Schopenhauer) also at the same time effectuates the temporal existence and condition of the individual soul. But what are we to think of as meant by such a mystical deed, an act through which the subject of it first comes into existence? Is it not this, that perhaps under this singular disguise there is concealed the simple thought that the origin of the bad lies not so much in a *doing* of the individual freedom as rather in the *rise* of it—that is to say, in the process of development through which the natural man becomes a moral man, and the merely potentially rational man becomes an actually rational man?

Let us, then, descend from the dangerous heights of transcendental speculation to the solid ground of experience, and let us try to discover the ground of the bad in the psychological presuppositions of the moral will. There is implanted in the nature of man a multiplicity of impulses of a lower and higher kind, which are at first all natural, neither good nor bad, but morally indifferent as it were, the raw material for the moral formation of the personal life. We distinguish as the chief kinds, the sensuous and the spiritual, the egoistic and the altruistic or social impulses. As the distinctive nature of man consists in his spiritual capacity, the sensuous impulses are destined to subordination under the spiritual impulses; and as the ends of society are of higher value than those of individuals, the egoistic impulses are destined to subordination under the social. But the state of man at the beginning does not correspond to this order, which is demanded by the rational nature of man. Because man as a natural being enters into existence with the mere capacity for rationality, the lower impulses preponderate over the higher in him from the beginning. This is natural, and in itself is not yet bad, but the germ of badness lies undoubtedly in this initial preponderating of the lower impulses. For as soon as the demands of reason, exhibited at first as commands of an external authority, are addressed to the child, forthwith there shows itself a discord between this obligation and his own will, which seeks to assert itself in its previous sensible and selfish direction. The real energy of the natural impulses does not immediately give way before the representations of the prohibiting foreign will, whose higher right at the beginning is not yet recognised, and at most is darkly felt. Nay more, the impulses disturbed in their naïve satisfaction by the prohibition, react at first the more strongly against the limitation enjoined upon them; and therefore the prohibition, instead of breaking the egoism of the self-will, rather incites it to defiant resistance and passionate appetency. Thus the man awaking to moral consciousness, finds himself from the beginning in a direction of will opposed to moral obligation; he finds in himself the propensity of a self-willed resistance to the moral order, which precedes all free action. This is the "radical badness," which therefore has its ground simply in the fact, that in the development of man out of naturality the lower impulses have already won a power of self-assertion and resistance before the reason could yet come to its valid position and authority. As this propensity of the self-will is grounded in the specific nature of man, it may be designated as inborn, hereditary, or "original" sinfulness. This universal propensity is further supplemented by the particular unfavourable predispositions which consist in an abnormal strength or weakness of one or other inclination, by which the moral order of life is sensibly made more difficult from the outset.

These particular unfavourable dispositions likewise rest upon hereditariness, and are therefore to be reckoned as belonging to the innate abnormity or "original sin." And, finally, there are combined with the innate evil many other kinds of acquired evils— bad examples of the surrounding society, and a false order of society, with conditions that make life more difficult for whole social classes, by which the impulse of self-preservation and liberty is inevitably incited to help itself by force or cunning, in the aggravated struggle for existence. All moral abnormities in the social institutions, practices, dogmas, and opinions, all the errors and wrong tendencies involved in the want of culture or of hyperculture, work with a morally depraving influence upon the education and development of individuals. The innate abnormity is thus heightened in manifold ways by acquired errors due to history; and all this together forms a morally abnormal habit of the will, which, taking precedence of all free acts, puts the man under the governing power of the bad. This tangled web of evil dispositions, woven as it is out of many threads, forms what the doctrine of the Church has designated "original sin," and what Kant has called "radical badness." The earnest truth expressed in these conceptions, which is entirely independent of the mythical Fall of Adam, ought least of all to be denied or mistaken by our time, which everywhere lays such great emphasis upon the solidarity of individuals with their social *milieu*, and upon their "hereditary burden."

On the other hand, the ecclesiastical judgment of the natural man suffers from exaggeration and excess, which is mainly to blame for the fact that its true kernel has been so frequently rejected. It is an exaggeration when original sin is considered as personally imputable guilt; and it is going too far when it is held to be the whole state of the natural man, and yet the actually present good, the "original grace," is overlooked. That can only be imputed to man as "guilt" which is grounded in his own self-determination; and this is just what original sin is not, seeing that it has its ground beyond the individual being and will, or at least beyond his conscious moral self-activity. In so far as it is grounded in the universal generic *nature*, it could not be designated at all as guilt, but only as disease (*vitium*). Yet in this pure naturalness it never occurs in reality, but always in some form or other of historical development, and consequently as a mixed product of nature and of the activity of earlier generations. In so far as the latter participates in it, the sinfulness of society at any time is a consequence of earlier actual sin and guilt, and consequently is itself also actual sin and guilt, only not of the individual, who gets it as an evil inheritance from his ancestors, but of the whole of mankind who have co-operated in its production for generations. Hence we may say with Schleiermacher, that original sin is the common deed and common guilt of the human race. But the individual always participates in this collective guilt in the measure in which he also takes part with his personal doing in the collective act that is directed to the furtherance of the bad. And this happens up to a certain degree inevitably in the case of every individual, who, having been born into the sinful society, grows up under its influence to moral responsibility. Then the inherited badness will always carry itself on in his own willing and doing, which, in so far as it is known as what ought not to be, is to be imputed to him as his own actual sin and guilt. In the conflict of the good and evil principles, which begins immediately with the first demands of moral authority, it is not possible that the good can always conquer from the beginning, as the yet wholly undeveloped reason stands powerless in opposition to the sensuous selfish inclination. Reason can only gradually become strong in conflict with the irrational natural impulse, while the inborn good germs are developed through the educating influence of the good, which is present in society. For, as on the side of the bad the individual does not stand upon his own footing alone, but carries part of the burden of sin and guilt which is accumulated in society as the inheritance from past generations, so neither on the side of the good has he been consigned merely to his own natural power and capacity, but he is supported and borne up by the common spirit of the good, which has formed itself in the moral community under the divine education of mankind as a historical inheritance from the past, and which in the advancing conflict against the ungodly forces authenticates itself as the victorious, world-conquering power. It is essential to the religious point of view to think of the conflict of the good and evil principle, not as an individual process proceeding exclusively in the individual soul and depending on the subjective force of the free will, but to regard it as a universal world-conflict passing down through history, a conflict which God's spirit itself carries on against all ungodly work and being, not outside of humanity but in it and through it, and by creating and preserving a community of goodness and of the good as a bulwark and weapon against the bad. And hence the Christian combines with the humble consciousness of his own weakness courageous confidence in the power of God, which is mighty in the weak. The utterance of the Psalmist concerning man's lowliness and dignity from which we started to-day, finds confirmation and deeper emphasis in the words of the apostle, "Not that we are sufficient of ourselves to think any thing as of ourselves; but our sufficiency is of God" (2 Cor. iii. 5).

LECTURE VIII.

THE RELIGIOUS VIEW OF MAN.

II. REDEMPTION AND EDUCATION.

IF it is essential to man to form ideals of a perfect life, and if he see himself continually impeded in their attainment by the resisting reality of things, he inevitably turns his hoping gaze towards the higher divine power, and expects from that power redemption from the evils which oppress him, and help to enable him to attain to his ideals. The hope of a redemptive manifestation of the Deity, and the striving to bring it about, are therefore found in all religions as an essential object of their faith and an essential motive of their worship. Whatever may be the nature of the hope of redemption, and by whatever conduct on the human side it is to be brought about, in every case it depends on the way in which the Ideal is thought; and this again is dependent on the stage of the moral development of men which has at any time been reached.

It is self-evident that, on the stage of nature-religion, redemption does not yet refer to the moral evil in man, but to the external evils in nature, which are regarded as punishments by the enraged Deity for the violation of his commands. To reconcile the wrath of the Deity by compensating performances or by voluntary expiations which discharge the penalty—it is to this that are referred the manifold expiatory practices, sacrifices, ceremonies of purification, fastings, mortifications, and mutilations which we find everywhere in the forms of worship in which the presuppositions of the nature-religions regarding the angry Deity still reign, or have a continued influence. In so far as the wrath of the Gods is to be referred to failures of religious observances—*i.e.*, to the violation of the private rights personally belonging to the Gods—so far do the means of expiating their wrath also move entirely in the sphere of ceremonial performances and penances, and are morally indifferent, or even anti-moral, as in the case of human sacrifices. But in so far as the Gods, in their capacity as representatives and protectors of the commonwealth, are also made angry by crimes against the social order of the community, the need of expiation extends to moral as well as to ceremonial trespasses, and it operates as a powerful motive to the consolidation of the civil order of right. The mixing without distinction of ceremonial and moral precepts is, as is well known, a common mark of all the oldest legislations.

The further development then proceeds in the direction that the moral is placed in significance above the ceremonial by the enlightened wise men and seers, and the possibility of an undoing of moral crimes by mere ceremonial performances is denied. The gradual distinction of the moral from the ceremonial, the repression and ultimate substitution of ceremonial expiation by the moral purification of the sense and life, and consequently the transformation of the mystical conception of redemption into the corresponding ethical conception of education, may be designated as the kernel and the teleological principle of the development of the history of religion.

Anticipatory divinations of this higher ethical idea of redemption are, however, already found on the basis of nature-religion under the covering of symbolically significant legends. For example, the legends of the sacrificial deaths of Codrus and Curtius in order to purchase the victory of their armies, rest indeed upon very superstitious representations of the wrath of the Deity, which was only to be reconciled by a voluntary human sacrifice; but they contain, nevertheless, the true thought that a redeeming power bringing salvation lies in the heroic sense of one who is prepared to sacrifice his own life for the good of his fellows. We may also here specially recall the profound myth of Heracles, the "hero and liberator," sprung from the Gods, who proved his power under conflicts and sufferings in the service of troubled humanity, and who obtained as the reward of his victory elevation among the Olympians. He is the opposite of Prometheus. As the latter is the man at variance with God, who by titanic self-will falls into guilt and calamity, so is Heracles the man allied with God, who remains obedient to his divine mission under all the trials of the earthly life, and who wins thereby the victory, and this not for himself merely, but for the bound Prometheus he also effectuates redemption from his torture and reconciliation with Zeus. It is the idea of the first and second Adam which we find here preindicated in mythical traits. How very natural it was to find in this mythical God-man the symbolical embodiment of the moral idea of redemption, is proved by the fable of Prodicus, in which Heracles becomes the hero of moral self-conquest who prefers the toilsome way of virtue to that of base enjoyment.

The thought illustrated in this fable, that salvation lies in the self-conquest of the will that is guided by reason, forms the theme of the practical philosophy of the Greeks from Socrates onwards. In Plato, however, this thought obtains the ascetic turn that the soul of man springs from the supersensible world, and is not truly at home in the earthly body, but is held in it as in banishment, in a prison, or in a grave. Hence man's task is to strive for redemption from this imprisonment by raising himself with all his thinking and striving out of the limits of the senses into the eternal world of thoughts. The true life of the wise man is a constant flight from the sphere of sense, and is therefore a preparation for death, in which this very return of the soul to its true life, which has already been spiritually striven after, finds its fulfilment, as is illustrated by the example of Socrates. With the Stoics this transcendent goal of the Platonic doctrine of redemption retreats into the background; but the practical ground-thought is still quite similar to that of Plato—namely, that man can only attain to satisfaction by making himself free from all passions, by ridding himself of all interests which bind him to the external world and to society, and by finding his immovable rest and lofty freedom in the pure inwardness of his own void self-consciousness. The Stoical ideal, as well as the Platonic, thus lies in the ascetic liberation of the Ego from what forms the subject-matter of life in the real world. Finally, in the Neo-Pythagorean and Neo-Platonic philosophy, this dualistic asceticism has become entirely transcendental mysticism, whose contempt of the world formed the exact opposite to the culture-ideals of the Greeks of the classical time with its joyous sense of the world. The world of sense, formerly full of the Gods, appeared now to be a thing without essence and worth, an unreal and agonising dream. Redemption from it and union with the world beyond—the world of purely spiritual and divine life

— had become the goal of man's longing, which he sought to approach by all the ways available to him, —theoretically, through the abstraction of thinking; practically, through the desensualising of the will; and mystically, through ecstasy of feeling.

A similar process, with a similar result, had, however, already been passed through, several centuries earlier, in India. By the way of continued abstraction the Brahmanic philosophy had come to regard the world of sense as an essenceless appearance, as the "deception of Maya," from which the wise man had to release himself, partly through practical asceticism, and partly through the deeper knowledge of the All-unity of Brahma. The blessedness of the wise man is described by the Vedanta philosophy in terms quite similar to those used by the Stoics: No care about the things of the world any longer troubles him who recognises the world as an illusion; no pain, even of his own body, any longer affects him who is able to recognise his own body as an illusion. The incorporeal and unchangeable being, as the wise man has come to know himself to be, is no more affected by pleasure and pain; even the fruit of earlier works, of the good as well as the bad, is done away with for the consciousness of the wise man. For him who has recognised the self as the unchangeable, and consequently also the non-active being, the earlier works which he has performed under the delusion of being an actor turn to nothingness when this illusion is taken away. But the same knowledge which makes the earlier sins an illusion annuls also the good works, past and future.

> "He who in himself his peace has found,
> Is by no duty ever henceforth bound."

With the knowledge of the unity of the Self with the All-One, all willing and obligation have come to an end. Thus does rest reign in the soul of him who is redeemed by knowledge, but it is the rest of death, of the dead and emptied heart, to which the goods as well as the evils of life, the true ends and ideals of life as well as the false ones, have become null and vain, and life has thus been robbed of all true worth. To one thus inwardly dead the outer life still rolls purposelessly on for a while, although without a definite end, as the potter's wheel continues to revolve after it has once received an impulse. But when at last what remains of the natural impulse of life has been consumed, the spirits of life no longer move forth into new existence, and the redemption of the wise man is completed by his entire dissolution into the All-One. From the same mood of weariness of the world and longing for death also proceeded the doctrine of redemption of Gautama Buddha. It theoretically drew the consequences of the Brahmanic Pantheism, and practically made the way to redemption accessible to all, and it raised the ascetic ideal of life to a common rule for an organised fellowship. The Buddhistic doctrine of redemption is comprised in the four "sacred truths" of suffering, of the origin of suffering, of the removal of suffering, and of the way to the removal of suffering. That all life is only suffering, because all that lives is subjected to constant change, because all things arise only in order to perish again, and perish in order to return again to a new circle of purposeless and painful existence—this is the fundamental theme of the Buddhistic preaching. But the ground of this endless suffering lies in the thirst of the soul for pleasures, for the enjoyment of life, and for power. Suffering lasts as long as the Ego that wills cleaves to the world of the becoming, which is subject to the laws of causality and of transitoriness. But what chains the will to existence is its not-knowing of the nothingness of all existence: when this not-knowing ceases, the man comes to the knowledge of the eternal law which condemns all willing to endless suffering, and then his will ceases to cling to the finite. With the insight into the aimlessness and vainness of all desire after happiness, the desire itself is quenched; and consequently suffering is also at an end, and deep peace takes its place. The final goal is then reached—namely, "Nirvâna," the extinguishing of the will which strives after life. "The disciple who has got rid of pleasure and desire, he who is rich in wisdom, has here below reached redemption from death, has attained rest, Nirvâna, the eternal place. He who has escaped from the impassable, hard, deceptive path of the Samsara—*i.e.*, of the circling round of the becoming—he who has crossed over and reached the shore, who has sunk into himself without wavering and doubt, who has delivered himself from the earthly and attained to Nirvâna,— him I call a true Brahman." So runs one of the sayings of Buddha, collected in the Dammapada. The ideal of the Buddhistic redemption is therefore the state of the soul which is released from joy and sorrow, fear and hope, which has divested itself of all wishes and purposes, which has found the rest of full renunciation in the knowledge of the nothingness of the world and its own existence; and this ideal is therefore at bottom essentially the same as the Stoical apathy, and as the Neo-Platonic flight from the world and emptying of the consciousness of all definite contents until complete ecstasy is reached, which is in fact an extinguishing of the conscious Ego, at least a temporary Nirvâna.

This is the *negative redemption*, which we may regard as an imperfect preliminary stage in the education of humanity to the true positive redemption. That it is not without a relative truth will be admitted by every one who knows the near affinity of many Buddhistic sayings regarding the vanity of earthly things with passages in the Bible. If man was to come to his true divine destination, he must recognise as nothingness and vanity the sensuous selfish purposes of the natural life—both of the narrowest personal and of the widest national egoism, which in their antagonism to one another continually cross and annul each other. This recognition was the result of the ancient development of culture, which had proceeded from the selfish eudæmonism of the individuals and of their natural associations; and the knowledge of the insufficiency of these impure and limited ideals of the natural selfish eudæmonism was the necessary preparation for elevation to the true all-embracing ideal that could make all happy. The defect, however, of this ascetic doctrine of redemption was, that it stopped at negation without being able to find its positive completion. In contrast to the naïve optimism of the natural eudæmonistic affirmation of the world, the pessimistic negation of the world was a necessary step in advance: its error, however, was that it stopped at the negation of the natural selfish purposes, and did not rise to the true universal life-purpose of humanity united in God, to a positive highest good, in which even the finite goods are again embraced as members of the whole and rightly put into order. We also believe that the world with its fashion passes away, but we know at the same time that he who does the will of God abideth for ever, and that our faith is the victory which has overcome the world. This true positive redemption, prepared in the religion of Israel, has come to fulfilment in Christianity.

The religion of Israel, from the time of the prophets, was practical idealism; its fundamental characteristic was the hope of a future time of salvation, in which the ideal of a just and happy people of God was to be realised. That this ideal was not merely a subjective wish, but the highest truth, was immediately contained in the belief of the prophets in Jehovah, the just and almighty God of Israel, and the disposer of the fates of the peoples. But as the reality never corresponded to that ideal, either in respect of the moral state of Israel or in respect of its circumstances of happiness, there thus followed from the belief of the prophets in God the confident hope that God, by future proofs of His righteousness and strength, would redeem His people from all the evils of the present, inner and outer, moral and natural. This prophetic hope assumed many forms, according to the change of the historical position of Israel; but there were always combined in it these two sides: (1) The expectation that God would purify His people inwardly by a fearful day of judgment, and that He would help on the cause of the pious and righteous to victory and permanence; (2) the expectation that the people, thus purified and become pleasing to God, would then also be victorious over their external enemies, and would rejoice in the efflorescence of a period of national power and glory which should surpass the fairest memories of the flourishing time of David. The former ethical side of the prophetic hope of salvation was the germ of a rich future, while its earthly national side was the perishing husk, which was partly stripped off and partly transformed by the advance of the history of the Jewish people. When the national hopes were baffled in the Exile, and under the continuing foreign government of the centuries after the Exile, the popular religion of the prophets became the heart-religion of pious individuals, as it is expressed in the touching songs of the Psalmists. The redemption which the prophets had hoped for from a future revelation of the power and righteousness of Jahve for the whole of the people, the pious individual now hoped to experience in his personal life. The undeceptions produced by the bitter reality did indeed lead individuals, like the author of Ecclesiastes, to grave doubts; but to others they became the occasion of an ever deeper and purer apprehension of the idea of Redemption. To the pious man who consoled himself under external suffering with the fellowship of his God, this inner happiness became such a paramount good that he "asked nothing of heaven and earth" (Ps. lxxiii.) Here the hope of external salvation vanishes in the certainty of the pious man that in his love of God he already inwardly possesses freedom from the world. Yet this mystical forgetting of the world in the soul bound up with God, as it occurs here and there in the Psalms, never became, in the case of the pious Jews, the one-sided world-negation of the Indians, nor apathetic indifference to the moral life of the community. For the God of Israel is the positive will of goodness, who reveals Himself, not merely in pious hearts, but also in the guidance of the course of the world, as He who will overcome wrong and establish right. The pious Jew, in believing in this end of the divine government of the world, feels himself called to co-operation in this divine purpose; hence he can never isolate himself in one-sided quietistic inwardness, but always keeps his look open towards the whole of the people of God; "he waits for the consolation of Israel." Under this point of view even the sufferings of the pious obtain a new profound meaning; they appear as the means by which God will not merely prove and purify the pious man himself, but also work out the redemption of the sinful people. The patient suffering of the "Servant of God" is (according to Isaiah, chap. lviii.) the ransom by which the salvation of the people is purchased, the propitiatory sacrifice by which the guilt of others is overcome and repaired. This thought, the fruit of the experiences in suffering of the pious in the Exile, obtained new confirmation under the persecutions and conflicts of the time of the Maccabees. The blood of the heroes of faith had not flowed in vain; it saved to the Jewish people their faith, and had even restored to them for a short time their political independence. From that time it became a universal doctrine of the Jewish theology that the innocent suffering, and especially the martyr-death, of the just, has an expiating and redeeming efficacy for the whole people. Contemporaneously with the view that the suffering of the just does not stand in contradiction with the hope of redemption, but is rather a means of its realisation, this hope itself rose above the earthly life to transcendent heights. Isaiah had already said of the Servant of the Lord, " When Thou shalt make his soul an offering for sin, he shall see his seed, he shall prolong his days, and the pleasure of the Lord shall prosper in his hand" (liii. 10). And these words suggested the expectation that the pious martyrs will have a share, even personally, in the victory of their cause, by means of a resurrection from the dead. Influences of the Persian religion worked in the same direction, and so it came that, from the age of the Maccabees, the belief in the resurrection of the just grew up among the Jewish people; and thereby the idea of the future time of salvation was transported generally from the soil of the natural world, and raised into the supernatural. The more the reality always again fell short of their high-strung expectations, the more difficult it was to think of the fulfilment of the prophetic ideals taking place in the natural way of historical development, so much the more boldly did the gaze of the Apocalyptic seer raise itself to the heavenly heights. According to the revelations of Daniel and Enoch, the kingdom of the saints and the elect was to descend to the earth upon the clouds of heaven and accompanied by heavenly hosts, and as a *new world* which was to be brought in by catastrophes of divine omnipotence and to take the place of the present world, which is governed by demons. Thus also among the Jews the place of the once optimistic idealism of the prophets was taken by a pessimistic despair of the real world, and of the possibility of a redemption of it by the natural way of history. The Jewish dualism of the present and of the future world corresponded to the Greek dualism of the sensible and ideal world; both were the manifestation of a resigned turning away from a reality that had become spiritless and godless. But in thus viewing them, the essential distinction is not to be left out of consideration that the Greek vainly longed for a bridging over of the abyss which separated the sensible world from the spiritual world, whereas the pious Jew cherished the hope of the coming of the future world through an act of divine omnipotence, and in this trusting hope he in the meantime inwardly anticipated the happiness of the future external redemption. On the one side the Phariseeac-apocalyptic hope of the miraculous coming down of the kingdom of God from heaven to earth, and on the other side the individualistic piety of the Psalmists and of "them that are quiet in the land," who, being satisfied in their fellowship with God, ask nothing of heaven and earth,—these were the two sides into which the historical-national hope of redemption of the prophets had resolved itself in the last pre-Christian century of Judaism.

These two sides of the Jewish piety — the individualism of the heart-religion of the Psalms, and the socialism of the prophetic-apocalyptic idea of the kingdom — were combined in Jesus of Nazareth into the unity of a unique religious geniality. The intimate union with God of the pious poets of the Psalms was the ground-tone of His religious life; to Him it clothed itself in the image of the most natural and most intimate human bond of fellowship—the image of the relationship of father and child. But this intimate union with God did not make Him indifferent to the world or to the needs of His people, for He saw in God not merely His Father, but the Father of all men; and He believed in the destination of all men to become actual children of God through trust in God and assimilation to Him. Thus heart-felt love to God became for Him the motive of active and patient love to the brethren; it constrained Him to offer the rest and joyfulness which he possessed in the consciousness of His sonship to God, to all who were weary and heavy laden, as a means of consolation and salvation. He turned with preference to those who were physically and spiritually sick, and sought by the exhortation of humble and trusting love to awaken and animate in them the glimmering spark of their better selves. His love awakened love in return; His trust in God awakened the courage of faith, before which the evil spirits of sin and insanity fled away; and thus did the humble and meek Teacher become the Physician of the sick, the Leader of the blind and strayed, the Deliverer of the captives. While He recognised in these results proofs of the victorious power of the divine spirit, the hope of the early coming of the kingdom of God became to Him a certainty that its existence had already begun. Although the apocalyptic expectation of a miraculous new order of all things and the inversion of all social relationships might still retain their hold even for Jesus, yet it was only the popular form in which a new thought of great reach clothed itself—namely, the thought that the coming of the kingdom of God proceeds *from within outwards*, that it has its first realisation in the hearts of men who feel and conduct themselves as children of the heavenly Father and as brethren towards each other, and that through the constant and quiet development of these inwardly acting powers of life even all that is external is gradually transformed, and the perfect time of salvation, if not directly accomplished, is at least introduced and prepared. When Jesus beheld in man the growing child of God, and in the world the growing kingdom of God, he did away the idle waiting for future redeeming miracles of Omnipotence and inaugurated the devoted working for the present *inward redemption*,—

that is, *education* of men into true children of God. In selfless devotion to this common task lay now the sole condition and surety of the participation of every one in the common good which God has prepared for His children, the kingdom of God. All the individual commandments of the law retreat into the background as meaningless before the one all-embracing command, "Love God with all thy heart, and thy neighbour as thyself!" "Seek ye first the kingdom of God and His righteousness!" With the greatness of the ideal goal grows also the demand upon willingness for sacrifice and the capability of performance on the part of man. For the highest good, all subordinate goods, and even one's own self, must be sacrificed; self-will and selfishness in every form must be overcome. But what makes this demand, which appears so hard, again an easy yoke and a light burden, is the certainty that the way of the Cross, that of the mortification of the natural selfish Ego, is only the way to the life of the true Godlike Ego: "Whosoever shall seek to save his life shall lose it; and whosoever shall lose his life shall preserve it." This is the kernel of the redeeming truth which Jesus has revealed, not through His doctrine merely, but also, and most of all, through His life and death. Thereby Jesus has become the Redeemer ($\kappa\alpha\tau$' $\dot{\epsilon}\xi o\chi\acute{\eta}\nu$) in that He first understood redemption in its true moral sense as the freedom in God which is to be realised by surrender of one's own will, and has presented it to the eyes of mankind typically in His person and in His life and death. All belief in redemption was henceforth to be tested by this ideal model.

As it is the fate of all new ideas that they must attach themselves to traditional notions, and under their garb obtain acceptance among men, but at the same time must lose much of their purity, so has it also fared with the Christian doctrine of redemption from the beginning. Already in the theology of the apostle Paul its dogmatic envelopment began with redemption being exclusively attached to the death of Jesus, and this death was set forth under the point of view of a vicarious expiation. This is easily explained from the personal relations of the apostle Paul. As he had not known Jesus in His lifetime, the teaching and life of Jesus could not make a decisive impression upon him; his whole interest was therefore concentrated from the outset on the death of Jesus. The death of the Cross had been to him at first the offence which prevented him from believing in the Messiahship of Jesus; but after the vision at Damascus this very death became to him the chief thing in Christ, the end of His divine mission, and the means of His work of redemption. The question, in what sense the death on the Cross could be the means of the Messianic redemption, found its answer to him simply from the presuppositions of the

Pharisccac theology, which beheld in the innocent suffering, and especially in the martyr-death, of the righteous, an expiatory means compensating for the sins of the whole people. What could be more natural than that Paul, from the moment when he recognised Jesus as the Messiah, should contemplate the death on the Cross from the same point of view as an expiatory means of salvation for the redemption of the sinful world? But it was not merely to the Jewish people that the expiatory effect of the death of Christ would extend, seeing that Jesus, according to the conviction of Paul, was not merely the Jewish Messiah, but the heavenly man, the ideal of men coming down from heaven, the second Adam. Hence the martyr-death of Jesus which had been suffered in obedience to the will of the Father, was accepted by Him as an expiation performed by the representative of humanity for all, by which the world had been reconciled with God; and His resurrection was regarded as the beginning of the new life of a regenerated humanity. In one respect this view may be made to appear as if redemption had again become a supernatural miracle, a mysterious expiatory sacrifice, which God Himself has carried into effect in the bloody death of His Son for the world, in order thereby to surpass and to supersede all previous sacrifices; and it is not to be denied that this more or less magical notion of redemption has played a great part in the Christian world. But let us not overlook the fact that under this dogmatic shell there is still concealed the same ethical kernel which we have recognised as the thought of redemption in the mind of Jesus. For what gives the death of Jesus its expiatory power is also, according to Paul, the mind of the ideal Man and Son of God, who sought not His own, who did not wish to seize His Messianic Lordship by violence, but merited it by means of His self-humiliation and obedience to death, even to the death on the Cross (Phil. ii. 7, 8). And the saving power of the death of Christ only comes into operation in those who enter in faith into the fellowship of His spiritual life,—who spiritually die and rise again with Him. Regarded from this point of view, Christ's death and resurrection have therefore the significance of a dramatic symbolising of the cardinal ethical truth, that it is the self-sacrifice of obedience and love by which man is released from sin and guilt, and becomes participative of the peace and freedom of a child of God. In this, therefore, Paul and Jesus entirely agree; the distinction between them is only this, that Jesus taught the redeeming truth immediately by His words and life, whereas Paul has enveloped it in the dogmatic notion of the sacrificial death of Christ suffered once for all *for us*, which must be carried on in advancing ethical self-sacrifice *in us*.

In the Church the dogmatic-supranaturalistic and

the ethical doctrine of redemption always held their place in its history side by side with each other, although the former stood more prominently in the foreground, not merely in the popular view, but also among the theologians. Its most widely spread form, which ruled for more than a thousand years, was the mythical representation of a conflict or juridical transaction between Christ and the devil—a fruitful theme for the medieval fantasy, and exhibited in manifold variations in art and legend. Yet this myth could not satisfy the more earnest-thinking; and hence the scholastic Anselm set himself the task, how to understand redemption, without reference to the devil, as the satisfaction of the God-Man required by the violated honour of God. His theory rested throughout on the presupposition of the secular and ecclesiastical morals of his time: the violated honour of God demands punishment or satisfaction. The punishment can be commuted by a performance of value, which, in the case of the debtor who is unable to pay, can be discharged by a kinsman. The death of the God-Man was regarded as an *opus supererogativum* of infinite meritorious value. This merit demands a corresponding reward, which is credited to the account of the human kinsmen of the God-Man, so as to cover their insufficiency in moral performances. The work of Christ, as Anselm construed it, was in fact nothing else than the prototype of the meritorious performances and satisfactions of the ecclesiastical saints, and was therefore from the standpoint of the medieval Church thought out quite logically. All the more remarkable is it that the Churches of the Reformation could be satisfied with this theory, notwithstanding that it stood in complete contradiction to their deeper moral consciousness. If, according to Protestant principles generally, there are no supererogatory meritorious works, then one would suppose that such cannot be accepted even in the case of Jesus. And if it is only the personal state of mind of the individual that decides regarding his salvation (which is the kernel of the doctrine of justifying faith), then one would suppose that there cannot be any vicarious performances of one for others at all, nor consequently any such even in the relationship of Christ to us.

These objections to the ecclesiastical dogma of redemption were already raised in the time of the Reformation by men like Schwenkfeld, Weigel, and Frank. "Our redemption," said Weigel, "rests not upon what the earthly Christ has done for us, as if we could help ourselves without repentance with His imputed righteousness. The life of Christ *in thee* must do it: Christ's death is imputed to no one; let him then have the death of Christ in himself, in the crucifixion of his old man." According to Frank, the historical Christ is given to us for an example and a sign of grace, that we may lay hold of God in Him. In Christ that becomes revealed which was formerly existing unconsciously in the hearts of the pious. But the history of Christ must consummate itself in all His members; the Word must also become flesh in us, must suffer and die and rise again in us. The intention of these really evangelically thinking men, to put an ethical and internal redemption in place of the dogmatic and external redemption, could not at first be carried through in opposition to the new dogmatism of the Protestant theology, but we may see in them the precursors of the idealistic philosophy of religion, which since Kant has exercised deep influence even upon the theological doctrine of redemption. According to Kant, belief in a mere historical proposition is dead in itself, and is of no avail for salvation : the proper object of the belief in Christ is the ideal Son of God—*i.e.*, the ideal of the humanity that is well-pleasing to God. This idea has the basis of its truth and binding power in the practical reason, and is independent of all historical traditions ; but it is brought to efficient perception through the example of Jesus, whom we therefore may regard as if the ideal of the good had appeared bodily in Him, without our having nevertheless on that account to see in Him anything else than a true man: nay more, by presupposing His mystical Deity, the typicalness of His moral example would rather be destroyed. Even the dogmatic theory that the guilt of men is vicariously expiated by Christ's death cannot, according to Kant's conviction, be correct in the proper sense, because guilt, as the most personal of all things, is not transferable. We are thus led to see in this theory the symbolical presentment of the truth that the new man in us suffers as it were vicariously for the old man; for he takes upon himself the daily pain of self-subjugation, and bears guiltlessly in patience the manifold evils which the old man could not but necessarily impute to himself as punishment. Therefore, as Christ is the exemplification of the moral idea of man, so His death is the symbol of that moral process of painful self-subjugation in obedience and patience, in which the true inner redemption of man consists. In like manner Fichte said, the only proper means of salvation is the death of selfhood, death *with* Jesus, regeneration. This is the way we must go: the history of how it has been discovered and made plain is indeed otherwise good, but it gives no help to going. Christianity is not reached until that way of blessedness is recognised as the sole and whole way, and what is historical is to be given over to the understanding. If one is really united with God, it is quite indifferent by what way he has come to it; and it would be a very useless occupation to be always merely repeating to one's self the remembrance of the way, instead of living in the thing itself.

In this philosophical doctrine of redemption there lies a significant truth, along with a sensible defect. The truth is this, that redemption is not a miraculous process external to us, which was accomplished long ago and once for all by the sacrificial death of a God in our favour, but that it is a moral event happening within the soul which always repeats itself, the self-sacrifice of the will to God in obedience, love, and patience. This is just what we have learned to know as the sense of Jesus' doctrine of redemption; and this is also just what was the kernel of the Reformation doctrine of justifying faith, which indeed is nothing but self-surrender to the holy love of God. But the defect in the Kant-Fichtean doctrine of redemption consisted in this, that it limited this ethical process of transformation to the individual, and endeavoured to explain it from his subjective reason and freedom alone. In this view the decisive question remained unsolved—namely, how the individual was of himself to become able to release himself from his moral imprisonment and powerlessness, and to become a new morally free man. For by appealing to what ought to be, to the law of the good lying in the reason, the possibility of its realisation was not at all explained, seeing that the law by itself alone is able indeed to weigh us down and to condemn us, but not to lift us up and liberate us. Limited to the individual, the victory of the good principle over the bad always remains problematical, a thing of happy accident without real guarantee. Only when the moral individual knows himself to be the member of a community in which the good principle has actually become the ruling common spirit, and shows itself always efficient as the victorious power over the bad in the collective historical life, — only then is the possibility likewise given that the individual may himself also become good through the educating power of the good Spirit which lives in the community. This is just the Christian doctrine of redemption. According to it, the moral liberation and regeneration of the individual is not the effect of his own natural power, but the effect of the divine Spirit, who, from the beginning of human history, put forth His activity as the power educating to the good, and especially has created for Himself in the Christian community a permanent organ for the education of the peoples and of individuals. It was the moral individualism of Kant which prevented him from finding in the historically realised common spirit of the good the real force available for the individual becoming good.

The post-Kantian philosophy overcame this defect by its turning from subjective to objective or historic-social idealism. And from this higher point of view Schleiermacher has pre-eminently understood how to combine the internality of Kant's ethical doctrine of redemption with the historicity of the principle of redemption which proceeded from Jesus Christ and is active in the Christian community. According to Schleiermacher, redemption is not a transcendent miraculous process, but a religious moral process of consciousness, which lies in the sphere of our experience and corresponds to the laws of our nature. That the consciousness of God, which belongs, along with the sensibility, to the generic nature of man as a rational being, must become free from its initial suppression and attain dominion over the lower side of man— this, according to Schleiermacher, is grounded in the unity of the divine decree of creation and redemption, or of the order of the world; and it therefore followed as a consequence with inner necessity from the development of the rational capacity of man—as it is also, according to Kant, a demand grounded in our reason—that the good principle shall become lord over the bad principle. But whereas Kant derived this victory from the freedom of the subject, and consequently made it inexplicable, or at least wholly problematical, Schleiermacher, on the other hand, rightly recognised that the experience of the individual, in respect of the bad as well as in respect of the good, stands in causal connection with the joint experience of the community of which he is a member. The passing from the dominion of sin to the dominion of the consciousness of God, in which redemption just consists, cannot therefore have its sufficient ground in the individual, but can only be a consequence and imitative repetition of the fundamental and typical transition which has been effected in the common consciousness of humanity through the historical life-work of Jesus Christ. The perfection in principle of the consciousness of God in Jesus was the redeeming power which appeared in Him as personal life; and which, proceeding from Him, is present and active as the holy common spirit in Christendom. If it is true that the individual life is always the abbreviated repetition of the generic life, and that the actualisation of the human capacities in the individual is only effected everywhere on the ground of their actuality in society, then it was certainly a happy thought of Schleiermacher to expand the different states of the religious self-consciousness (unfreedom and liberation of the higher self) into phases of the development of all religious humanity. Thereby he broke through the narrow individualistic and non-historical horizon of the *Aufklärung*, and reconciled the inner self-certainty of the personal spirit with the historical common spirit of Christendom.

Upon the standpoint of this universal-historical doctrine of redemption (as we may call it by way of distinction from Kant's individualism), the good is not a mere ought-to-be, an ideal without reality, the realising of which was expected exclusively from the subjective will, which, however, could never become capable of its task. But the good is the universal-rational will or divine Logos which realises itself in the course of the history of humanity, the revelation of which has indeed attained its highest point in Christ, but is by no means limited to Him, rather going back to the beginning of our race. The rational capacity innate in us, that image of God in man, already rests upon our participating in the divine Logos, which John for that very reason calls quite generally "the light of men," the light "which lighteth every man." And thus every step in the development of this divine germ of humanity, every thought which rises to the light of truth, every good deed which furthers and preserves the moral order, is likewise a revelation of the divine spirit which redeems us from crude nature and educates us into the glorious liberty of the children of God.

Undoubtedly the central revelation of this spirit has been the religious life of humanity at all times; and in this sphere Jesus Christ is the central form towering above all else, and His life-work is the decisive turning-point, the regeneration of humanity, the redemption (κατ' ἐξοχήν). But this does not exclude the fact that we may also recognise in all the other benefactors of humanity who have accomplished what is great and fruitful in religion and morality, in art and science, in discoveries and inventions, redeeming heroes and instruments of the divine education of humanity. The collected fruit of all these deeds and sufferings, conflicts and sacrifices, which contributed to further the spiritual development of our race, forms the true "treasure of grace" which is transmitted as a most precious inheritance from generation to generation.

Every individual who is born into the world of Christian civilisation and reared in it, enters immediately into the enjoyment of this inestimable inheritance, which is laid into his cradle as an unmerited good, and, we may say, as a gracious gift of the love and wisdom that govern the world. Before the waking consciousness of the spirit of the child is able to grasp the thought of the good as law, duty, task, and ideal, it has already long got to feel the good as the present good of civilised life, and as the educating power of truth and love. There also springs out of this precious gift of "the grace of God that bringeth salvation" (Titus ii. 11) a correspondingly high task for every individual. But the impossible is not demanded, namely, that every one should proceed to create the good out of his own weak powers; he has only to give himself up willingly to the existing spirit of the good, to appropriate it to himself, to live into it, and to let himself be trained by it to true freedom, in order then to work co-operatingly with strengthened power for the furtherance of the common good. "What thou hast inherited from thy fathers, acquire it in order to possess it!" This advancing work of appropriating and communicating spiritual goods, of letting one's self be educated and educating others for the good, in this dedication of the whole self to the furtherance of the universal good, of the kingdom of God,—in this work consists the ethical redemption of all.

LECTURE IX.

THE RELIGIOUS VIEW OF THE WORLD.

I. IDEALISM AND NATURALISM.

THE thought that the world has its sole ground in God is regarded in the Monotheistic religions as an almost self-evident cardinal proposition. But the history of religion teaches that this thought only grew very gradually to maturity in the consciousness of men. The devotees of Nature-religion did not yet know it. As its Gods are themselves Nature-beings, they cannot be the ultimate ground of Nature, but they arise at the same time with it. Where men reflected in the sphere of the Nature-religions regarding the origin of the universe, they thought that the visible world, together with the Gods and spirits, had arisen of themselves out of original germs or material elements; their Cosmogony was one with their Theogony. The notion was widely spread of a world-egg which, having burst, became heaven and earth, and out of whose contents even the

Gods had arisen along with other beings. Or they thought of Chaos as being the first, that formless mass in which all the germs of life, and of Gods and men, are still together; and which then by gradual separation and combination of the individual forces, unfolded itself into the world of the Gods and of earthly beings. According to Hesiod's cosmogony, for example, there was in the beginning Chaos and Eros (the vital impulse). Chaos divided itself into Tartaros and the Earth, and Earth brought forth out of herself the Sky and the Ocean. Uranos, moved by the vital impulse, fertilised Gæa and begot the Titans and Cyclops, but was mutilated by the Titan Kronos, and deposed from his lordship. Yet neither was the lordship of Kronos lasting; for he too was only the wild purposeless and untamable nature-force which swallows again its own children. He was overpowered by the youngest of his sons, Zeus, who shared the lordship of the world with his brothers Poseidon and Aidoneus. But even Zeus had still to secure his lordship from the revolt of the giants, the successors of the Titans; and it was only with the conquest of these that the crude elementary forces of Nature were for ever subdued by the rational and harmonious ruling of the Olympians, those human Gods. Thus, according to Hesiod's cosmogony, the present world of the Gods and men is the last product of a gradual development of higher and higher formations out of the primal Chaos. The same thought was carried out by the Ionian Nature-philosophy, which made the world arise out of one or several elements through separation and combination, or constructed it out of compositions of the original simple atoms. The first of the Greek philosophers who represented the chaotic first matter as formed through the ordering understanding of God (the νοῦς) was Anaxagoras, whom Aristotle on that account called "the first sober one among drunken ones."

There is not unfrequently found in the mythology of the Nature-religions a combination of Theogony and a divine formation of matter in such a way that the Gods—whether all or some or one of them—are the first products of Chaos, but then they form the rest of the world out of it. Thus, for example, in the Indian mythology Prajapati proceeded out of the golden world-egg, and then became the creative former of the world. Likewise, in the Chaldean mythology the great Gods arose at first out of Chaos, and they then created the other Gods and the living beings of heaven and earth.

The doctrine first expressed among the Greeks by Anaxagoras, that the rational spirit is the world-ordering principle, is found outside of the Biblical religion only among the Persians whose legend of Creation has a close affinity with the Biblical account, and perhaps even exercised a historical influence upon it. According to the Zendavesta, the all-wise spirit Ahura created the world in so far as it is good by his excellent word, with the purpose of forming a bulwark between the hostile kingdoms of the uncreated light and the uncreated darkness. The Creation was accomplished in 365 days and in six acts, in the course of which were formed the heavens and the lights of heaven, water, earth, plants, beasts, and men. Every earthly class of beings is the copy of a heavenly ideal—that is, is the realising of a divine idea. Ahura made the first human pair grow out of a twin-tree, and he implanted in their bodies their pre-created souls. This creation of Ahura was, like himself, perfectly good and pure; but it was spoiled by the hostile spirit Ahriman (Angromainyu), who to the good everywhere added the bad and pernicious—the naïvest solution of the question regarding the origin of evil, in which the greatest difficulty of the abstract super-naturalistic doctrine of Creation lies.

Whereas Nature-religion made Nature the absolute principle out of which even the spiritual and divine was to arise, on the other hand the *Biblical* religion puts in the first place the supernatural Spirit of God as the omnipotent principle of all becoming, and explains the world from His will, which expressed itself in His word of command. Yet it is not exactly a Creation out of nothing that is taught even in Genesis, but a formation of the world out of the initial Chaos, which is consequently presupposed as formless matter present to the divine creative activity. The description in Genesis i. of the gradual separation of Chaos into light and darkness, above and below, wet and dry, and then of the filling up of these spheres of the world with their appurtenant living beings in the work of six days, has a close affinity with the Persian and Chaldean legend. It is a religious speculation in which reflection is already much further advanced than in the naïver narrative of Genesis ii. While in Genesis i. a uniform plan reigns, and the acts of Creation proceed in a teleological series of stages, in Genesis ii., on the other hand, the Creation begins with the formation of the man out of a clod of earth; and thereupon the Garden of Eden is planted for his dwelling-place, then the beasts are created as his helpers, and finally the woman was formed out of a rib of the man. Here no regular planned progress finds place, but what is most immediately necessary is only created as occasion required, and in it a defect always again exhibits itself, and this impels to further creating. Even the mode of the creating is represented still more naïvely: the beings are not called into existence by the simple word of command, but God Himself puts His hand to the work; He plants the garden, forms Adam out of the earth, breathes breath into his nostrils, frames Eve out of his rib, and afterwards makes for our first parents their first clothing out of skins. The striking naïveté of these ideas seemed to the Greek fathers to be a clear proof that this whole narrative was not meant to be taken literally but allegorically.

The *Christian* doctrine of Creation is distinguished from the Old Testament doctrine by the significant thought that the world was created through the divine Logos—by which is now no longer meant the mere word of command, but the divine Spirit which is active in the world, and which finds the culmination of its revelation in the Son of God, on which account the Son Himself is also designated as the Mediator and final end of the Creation (John i. 1; Heb. i. 2; Col. i. 16). The meaning of this New Testament doctrine is seldom understood in its far-reaching significance; and this is natural, because we are not accustomed to distinguish between the divine Logos and the man Jesus. Absurd as would be the notion that the world was created by and for Jesus, as profoundly true is the thought that it is a work of the divine reason which orders the chaos of forces from eternity to eternity, and guides the course of the development of the world to the final end of a moral kingdom of spirits. That the divine idea of man as "the son of His love," and of humanity as the kingdom of this Son of God (Col. i. 13), is the immanent final cause of all existence and development even in the prior world of Nature,—this has been the fundamental thought of the Christian Gnosis since the apostolic age, and I think that no philosophy has yet been able to shake or to surpass this thought—the

IDEALISM AND NATURALISM. 273

corner-stone of an idealistic view of the world. The whole idealistic philosophy of modern times is in fact only the carrying out and grounding of the conviction, that Nature is ordered by spirit and for spirit as a subservient means for its eternal ends; that it is therefore not, as the heathen naturalism thought, the one and all, the last and highest of things, but has the spirit and its moral ends over it as its lord and master. This is the true, the only genuine supernaturalism, which is just as far removed from the abstract Jewish supernaturalism as from the heathen naturalism. For if the Logos is the rational purposive thinking of God, the ordering power over Nature, then Nature is an ordered system of final thoughts, its process of becoming is a development from lower to higher, in the whole of which every individual thing has its determined place, and serves the whole according to the law of its kind. As the order of means for the ends of the spirit, as the causal mechanism for the teleological idea, Nature comes to its full right, asserts its inner conformity to law and purpose, and does not become the football of an external arbitrary will or the playground of a divine omnipotence whose "supernatural miracles" would put in the place of the real Nature an imaginary super-nature, which would be no Nature at all. The view of the world which alone truly corresponds to the principle of Christianity is this moral idealism, which perfectly accords with intellectual realism, being as far removed from the Jewish fantastic-apocalyptic supranaturalism as from the heathen spiritless and godless naturalism. These two extremes are the ever-threatening enemies of Christian truth, and to them are due, even in our own day, the conflicts between faith and knowledge.

The Church of the second century had to guard itself from the danger of falling back into heathen naturalism, a danger which threatened it from Gnosticism. In the course of this conflict, however, the Church itself fell into the abstract Jewish supernaturalism, to which it gave the harshest expression in the doctrine that the world was created out of nothing by a free act of the divine omnipotence in time—with which position the reality of Nature was as much put in question theoretically as its right was practically denied in Asceticism. The hostility to Nature of the medieval supernaturalistic Christianity was the opposite extreme to the naturalism of the ancient world. With the Renascence of the ancient culture, love of Nature, and consequently also the study of it, began to waken anew; and out of it arose the collisions between the science of Nature and the doctrine of Creation, which have never since ceased.

The discoveries of astronomy gave occasion to the first conflict. The Heliocentric system of the world of Copernicus appeared to the theologian Melanchthon, otherwise so mild, as a godless innovation which the government ought to suppress. It cannot be denied that in taking this view he showed more insight into the bearing of this innovation than do most of the theologians of our day, who are wont to ignore, or at least as far as possible to minimise, the antagonism between the Copernican and the Biblical or Geocentric view of the world. The opposition in fact affects not the Biblical history of Creation only, but its consequences reach still further. If the resting earth becomes a rolling globe, and the fixed vault of the heavens becomes the infinite space of the world, then for the religious fantasy, with the fixed *above* and *below*, disappears also the frame within which it had localised the chief acts of the divine-human drama of the history of salvation, from Paradise on till the second coming of Christ. But if the external theatre in space is withdrawn from these acts, they can no longer be represented as external events, and the necessity therefore appears imposed on the religious thinker to apprehend the divine revelation as not in space and not in sense, but as a spiritual process in the human consciousness. Further, when it is held that the earth is no longer to be regarded as the centre of the universe, the position of man in relation to the order of the whole appears also to be changed. As the inhabitant of a small province of the universe, he can no longer claim that the whole world should direct itself according to his wishes, that from regard to his wants the sun should stand still several hours, or the shadow of the sun-dial go backwards. When the conformity to law in the movement of the heavenly bodies was once recognised, it was a near consequence that the processes of earthly nature are also subject to the same conformity to law. The progress of mathematics and physics in the sixteenth and seventeenth centuries led to an entirely new conception of "Nature." The place of final causes was taken by mechanical causalism; the place of angels and demons and of arbitrary acts of omnipotence was taken by the universal inviolable law of the universe.

To this revolution in the view of nature philosophical expression was given by Spinoza. The keystone of his philosophy is the thought that God is the *causa immanens* of the world, and that the divine causality does not work with arbitrariness, but that all its operations follow as necessarily from its nature as the properties of the triangle do from its essence. Regarding the traditional conception of Creation, Spinoza judged that it turns God into arbitrariness, and the world into chance; and instead of it, according to him, God should be thought as the *natura naturans* which unfolds itself naturally in the *natura naturata*, just as every force unfolds itself in the totality of its effects. As long as men wish to find everywhere in nature the particular intentions of one governor or of several, who arbitrarily direct things with reference to the advantage or harm of men, so long is a sound knowledge of nature impossible. The delusive idea, that in all the processes of nature extramundane powers have their hand in play, and prosecute their particular intentions, is, according to Spinoza, an *asylum ignorantiæ* ministering to human selfishness, a superstition which makes men the slaves of their own imaginations and passions; and in opposition to which, the true piety consists in recognising God's revelation in the eternal laws of the world's order, and in accommodating one's self to it submissively. Certainly Spinoza was right in combating the abstract supernaturalism with its external and arbitrary directing of things according to particular intentions, and in energetically representing the conformity to law of all that happens in nature, which is the principle of modern science. But in his polemical zeal Spinoza shot beyond the mark in understanding the conformity to law of what happens so that it excludes all purposiveness, —a view in agreement with this other that he was able to apprehend God only as substance, as efficient force, and not as spirit or as active thought positing ends. The consequence of this was, that his view of the world had a wavering tendency towards a naturalism with which the Biblical idealism cannot be combined.

Leibnitz sought to remove this defect by thinking of nature as the system of both efficient causes and of final causes at once—the former according to its corporeal manifestation, the latter according to its inward psychical side. In like manner Leibnitz sought to understand God's causality as free and necessary at the same time, in so far as God has created the world as it is, not indeed with physical but with moral necessity, by choosing out of many possible worlds the best for actualisation. This position had the effect, not in the intention of Leibnitz himself, but according to the way in which it was apprehended by his followers, of opening the door anew to the Deistic separation of God from the world, and to the arbitrary teleology which then diffused itself and made itself ridiculous in the popular Physico-theology of the eighteenth century. Hence profounder minds like Lessing, Herder, and Goethe returned again to Spinoza, yet in such a way that they completed the abstract Monism of substance by Leibnitz's Monadology, and the ateleological causalism by Leibnitz's teleology. God is conceived as the spirit which inwardly moves and rules Nature, and Nature as the manifestation of His rational purposive thoughts, as "the living garment of the Deity" (Goethe). In Fichte's high-strung idealism Nature lost all reality, and became the mere representation of the mind, which in this image of its own imagination creates the material of its moral activity. For the rest, Fichte rejected as decidedly as Spinoza the supernaturalistic conception of Creation: he called it the fundamental error of all false metaphysics, a Jewish and heathen principle by which the conception of the

Deity is fundamentally corrupted, and invested with an arbitrariness which operates prejudicially upon the whole religious system. It was Fichte's conception of the moral world-order which excluded the lawless arbitrariness of the abstract super-naturalism. Schelling's nature-philosophy restored to nature its reality, but conceived of it as the means subservient to the ideal ends of the spirit which develops itself through the stages of the existence in nature in order to come to itself in man as spirit. Nature thus appears as the means posited by the spirit for the self-realisation of the spirit; and its becoming thus appears as the preliminary history of the development of the human spirit.

However much the philosophy of nature may have erred by arbitrary hypotheses and *a priori* constructions, yet this one merit must be conceded to it, that it first applied the great principle of *development* to nature, and thereby showed the way which can lead men beyond the antagonism of the traditional super-naturalism and the mechanism which reigned in the seventeenth and eighteenth centuries. The first who trod this so important way was Herder. In his 'Ideas for a Philosophy of History' he viewed man as the final goal to which the terrestrial organisation strove. Through the whole scale of beings, from the stone to the animal, and at last to man, the form of organisation rose higher and higher; the impulses and forces of the creatures became more multifarious in kind, and at last they were all combined in the form of man. The beasts, says Herder, are men's elder brothers, the prior stages upon which formative nature exhibited separately, in passing, what it wished to realise in man. Man can only obtain his lordship over the other creatures by combating for it. For all things are in conflict with each other, because all are hard beset. Every species cares for itself as if it were the only one; but at its side there stands another which restricts it to certain limits, and only in this relationship of opposite species did nature find the means for the preservation of the whole. It is only through the equilibrium of forces that peace comes about in the Creation. Herder therefore conceived the becoming of the terrestrial nature as a development of more and more complicated organisms out of simple organisms, a development in which even the conflict of living beings with each other, the "struggle for existence," played an essential part. The question, however, as to the How? of the proceeding of one form of life out of the other forms of life, still remained undetermined in the speculations of the nature-philosophers. This was supplemented and completed by the scientific investigators of nature. Lamarck, at the beginning of our century, taught that the various species had proceeded out of the simplest organisms, which had arisen by original generation through accommodation to the altered conditions of life; but he found no approval as yet in his own time. It was first through Darwin that the doctrine of development obtained prominent recognition. As is well known, he started from the observation that in the breeding of plants and animals great varieties of species can be attained by individuals possessing definite properties being used for propagation, whose specific peculiarity is then increased more and more by inheritance from generation to generation. From this he inferred that it was through a similar procedure in nature, called "Natural Selection," that all organic species had developed themselves out of an original fundamental form. Natural selection was explained by Darwin from the fact that in the universal struggle for existence, it is always only the individuals best adapted to their conditions of life that survive; and as these individuals transmit their peculiarly favourable qualifications to their descendants with a continuous increase of their peculiarity, the manifold species are thus formed in the course of generations out of the gradual accumulation of the specific differences.

The justification of this theory of natural science—which we, of course, have not to examine here in detail—appears to me to consist in this, that it is in full earnest with the thought of the development of all life. To every view that regards things as having been artificially made according to accidental designs, there is herewith opposed the insight that all that lives is a becoming from within through proper self-activity which unfolds the germs lying in a being according to its own law, and makes itself in actuality that for which the real potentiality lay in its nature. But at the same time there must always be presupposed an inner living impulse which strives after, not its preservation merely, but also its exertion and unfolding in a definite direction. This inner factor was not quite overlooked by Darwin, as he lays it at the very basis of the struggle for existence as well as of sexual attraction; but Darwin has ascribed less significance to this inner psychical principle than to the external conditions of life, from which he derived all variations. In this it appears to me that there lies a one-sidedness, which, however, does not affect the theory of development as such, but only the application to which it has been put, and this not so much by Darwin himself as rather by the successors of that great investigator of nature, in so far as it has been turned by them to account in order to found upon it a materialistic view of the world. The opinion prevailing on this point, that through the causal development of life all and every teleology is excluded, is a fatal error. That causality and teleology are rather the inseparably coherent sides of all organic life, was already known by Aristotle, and has been irrefutably shown by Leibnitz and Kant. What else, then, is the living impulse of a being which struggles for self-preservation in conflict with the external world, than a striving after the realisation of the possibility inherent in its essence, and therefore after an indwelling end? If, however, nature is a system of unconscious correlative final causes, or forces striving towards a goal, then it presupposes a universal purposive thought, and consequently an end-positing reason, as the organising purposive cause of the whole. If the Darwinian doctrine of development has been made use of in order by its aid to derive life itself from the primal matter, and to give an apparently scientific grounding to materialism, this has been an inconsiderate confounding of the most heterogeneous things. David Friedrich Strauss in his last book, 'The Old Faith and the New,' has set forth the opinion that motion may be transformed under certain circumstances as well into sensation as into heat; but Zeller has rightly objected to this view that the transmutation of motion into ideas not only lacks all relevant analogy, but that this assumption also involves the clear contradiction that the embracing of the manifold into the unity of consciousness would have to be explained without a single subject of consciousness. This is generally the cardinal error of all materialism, that it would explain the world out of mere states and processes of external objective being, and does not pause to think that we should know nothing at all of this being without a subjective consciousness, which is therefore to be always presupposed in our knowing of things, and therefore cannot be derived from it. How, then, could we know anything, even of the conformity to law of the motion of bodies, without our embracing the perceptions that follow each other in time, in the unity of an act of thought which presupposes a consciousness that continues identical with itself in the change of its ideas, and which refers the change of its contents to the identity of its self-activity? Moreover, it has been at length openly confessed by the more circumspect even among the investigators of nature, that it is impossible to explain sensation and consciousness, and therefore the actual human world itself, by materialistic presuppositions. With this all reason for any anxiety concerning the irreligious consequences of the doctrine of development falls away; but if its extravagances are set aside, we may with the more freedom from bias examine its true significance for the religious view of the world, and we may draw the balance of loss and gain resulting from it as regards the traditional supernaturalistic doctrine of creation.

And first of all, from the standpoint of the doctrine of development, the literal truth of the Biblical narrative of the six days' work of Creation—according to which the world has been called into existence "cut and dried" out of nothing, by means of certain divine miraculous acts — is a position which must be given up. Therewith we undoubtedly lose a convenient answer to the question regarding the *Whence* of the world, which seemed to be so simply solved by the six days' work. But yet only *seemed!* For it could not escape any one who reflected in any measure upon it that that answer was sketched from the standpoint of a still very childish view of the world, which our present knowledge has far outgrown. We need no longer enter upon the details of the Biblical history of Creation, after having shown its contradiction in principle with the Copernican system of the world. But even the dogmatic formulæ of the supernaturalistic doctrine of Creation are of no greater value. With the proposition that God has called the world out of nothing into existence, no positive thought can be connected. "Out of nothing comes nothing," or what appears to have come out of it has merely an apparent being; it is an enchanted nothing, an illusionary phantasm like the dream of Maya: but such a merely apparent existence cannot be seriously ascribed by us to the world, for we know at least that we ourselves and our fellow-men are something, and do not merely appear to be. We have also come to know God's being from His revelation in the order of the world; and if the reality of the world became doubtful to us, the being of God would also become subject to the same doubt, and then we would have to go through the same dialectic again, by which the Brahmanic Akosmism, that had explained the world as mere seeming, led to the Buddhistic Atheism.

Hence we cannot give up the reality of the world, both on account of our own selves and on account of the reality of God; and hence we cannot rest in the position that the world, having arisen out of nothing, is, as it were, an enchanted nothing. Much rather would we prefer to say with ancient Church fathers and modern philosophers, that the world has its substance from the will of God, and its form from the understanding of God. Further, a beginning and ending in time of the creating of God are not thinkable. That would be to suppose a change of creating and resting in God, which would equalise God's being with the changeable course of human life. Nor could it be conceived what should have hindered God from creating the world up to the beginning of His creating. If He had previously either not yet had the power or not the will to do it, He would have been in so far imperfect, and therefore not yet true God; but this would contradict the conception of His eternity and unchangeableness. But as regards the ending of Creation with the six days' work, this opinion is corrected by the doctrine of the Church itself, in so far as it designates the preservation of the world as a "continual creation," and consequently will not think of creation as concluded at any one time. Moreover, geology teaches us that the earth has passed through various periods of indefinitely long duration before it attained a formation of its surface that was fitted to be a dwelling-place for man; while astronomy teaches that in the universe there are always celestial bodies and even whole sun-systems still arising, and therefore that creation is not yet ended to-day. All this agrees in leading to the conclusion that we must give up the assumption of a creation that happened but once, and that has begun and ended in time; and instead of it we prefer to say rather with Scotus Erigena that the divine creating is equally eternal with His being. Hence the world thus viewed continues to be the region of temporal, changeable, and transitory being, even if this whole of risen and perishing parts has itself never begun nor will cease to exist. If we therefore put in the place of single supernaturalistic acts of creation rather the eternal and omnipresent activity of the divine omnipotence and omniscience in the world, then, as it seems to me, we have lost nothing at all for the religious view of the world, but we have won for science freedom to investigate the efficient causes and laws in the natural connection of things, without coming into collision with religious presuppositions, since the divine omnipotence, as eternally omnipresent, works not without but through the order of finite causes in conformity with law. What leads to the endless conflicts with natural science is not the idealism of the religious view of the world as such, but only its traditional investment in that abstract supernaturalism which makes omnipotence work as an anthropomorphic cause without and against the order of the whole. This anthropomorphic and miraculous supernaturalism invariably calls forth the reaction of naturalism, which then rejects with the mythical envelope also the true religious kernel, the lordship of the spirit over nature, and leads to the heathen deification of material existence. If we would protect ourselves from that unspiritual and godless naturalism, which in fact contains the greatest danger for religion and morality, we ought not to seek our refuge with the supernaturalism which puts God out of the world, and which on that account can never become truly master of naturalism, because it is at bottom itself only another refined form of it, in so far as it rears up a second fantastic nature above the real nature. Nay, we must rather seek escape from this "vicious circle" in the idealism of the truly religious view of the world, which finds the divine spirit everywhere present and active in the world,—*without* in nature as creative vital force, and *within* in our own heart as the voice of truth and love. This is what the apostle meant when he said, "He is not far from any one of us; for in Him we live and move and have our being." And it is what Goethe means in the classical passage: "What were a God who only gave the world a push from without, or let it spin round His finger? It is fitting for Him to move the world from within, to foster Nature in Himself, Himself in

Nature; so that whatever lives and moves and has its being in Him, never lacks His power or His spirit."[1]

A special objection to the doctrine of development is often raised with regard to the position of man in relation to the sub-human nature. If a continuous natural development between the sphere of nature below man and man is accepted, does not man then lose his distinguished position and distinguishing dignity, and is he not lowered to the level of the beasts? I can assign no great importance to this objection. The religious dignity of man rests, after all, in any case upon what he *is*, not upon the mode and manner in which he has *become* what he is. It is his rational capacity which makes him man, and distinguishes him from the beast; and this prerogative remains precisely the same in whatever way the entering of this rational being into terrestrial existence may be thought to have been brought about. Whether God immediately formed him out of a lump of earth — which is, after all, no peculiarly distinguished material — or caused him to be gradually developed out of unnumbered generations of the terrestrial Fauna, the one is no better and no worse than the other, and neither of them can occasion

---

[1] "Was wär ein Gott, der nur von aussen stiesse,
Im Kreis das All am Finger laufen liesse?
Ihm ziemt's die Welt im Innern zu bewegen,
Sich in Natur, Natur in Sich zu hegen,
So dass, was in Ihm lebt und webt und ist,
Nie seine Kraft, nie seinen Geist vermisst!"

any disparagement whatever to the dignity of man. We do not feel ourselves at all degraded by the fact that during our embryonic pre-existence we must pass through various forms of lower animal existence; why then should the human species be more ignoble if it lived through as many thousand years of preliminary animal stages upon earth before it entered into the appearance of man, as the individual now lives through days of embryonic animal pre-existence? Are not a thousand years before God as one day? Instead of the loss that is feared, the doctrine of development might rather indicate a gain for the position of humanity in the universe. If man is the crown of creation in the sense that the whole process of development in nature has striven towards his appearance, then he stands no longer in opposition to nature as to an alien and hostile power, but he recognises in it a fore-stage of his own life, a divining and yearning of the still unfree spirit in its animal state, for which the fulfilment and liberation has come, and will further come, in himself. Thus has the apostle Paul said that the whole creation groaneth and travaileth in pain together until now, and waiteth for the glorious freedom of the children of God. And thus did Jesus see in the natural life the likeness of the spiritual life, both of them governed by the same eternal laws of the divine world-order, revealing themselves in nature and in the life of man, only in different stages of their development. If the pious man finds everywhere in nature the signs and wonders of his God; if the poet sees in it the mirror of his own soul, and hears in its manifold voices the echo of his own joys and sorrows; if even the philosopher beholds in the starry heavens the image of the moral order of the world which lives in his heart,—all this is not mere arbitrary imagining, but it is the proper manifestation of the harmony of nature and spirit as eternally grounded in God. The reconciliation of these two things, long since recognised by Christianity in prophetic intuition, and expressed in the words " the incarnation of the Logos," has been raised to scientific knowledge in the modern doctrine of development.

In this spiritualised view of nature lies also a rich compensation for the loss of the supernatural *miracles*, which undoubtedly have no longer any place in a world of continuous development in conformity with law. Goethe has said that

"Miracle is faith's own dearest child."

And he is right; for miracle is for the childish view of the world the most natural expression of the conviction that the power of God reigns throughout the world and controls it. So long as the divine omnipotence is still represented in a natural fashion as an individual cause along with and above other causes, the religious consciousness clothes itself in the representation of individual miraculous operations which break through the familiar course of nature. Yet the boundary between miracles and nature is still a shifting one so long as the conformity of nature to law is not yet clearly known. It is with this knowledge that miracle first ceases to be a mere extraordinary occurrence, and becomes an absolutely supernatural miracle contrary to law. But as soon as the idea has obtained this significance, it is no longer tenable by any logical thinking, as all the philosophers since Spinoza have acknowledged. But even the religious faith, if it rightly understands itself, has no interest in maintaining the supernaturalist conception of miracle. Schleiermacher has strikingly remarked that in his judgment it cannot be seen how the divine omnipotence should show itself greater in the interruptions of the connection of nature than in the unchangeable course of it, which in fact also rests upon divine arrangement. Through every absolute miracle the whole connection of nature, both forwards and backwards, would be destroyed, and the conception of nature itself abolished; the divine activity would become an unordered magical mode of working; God would be co-ordinated with finite causes, and thereby even be made finite. On the other hand, when it is said as a defence of miracles that they are a sign of the livingness and freedom of God, it appears to be supposed that God is usually unliving and unfree, and comes only in the rare exceptional cases of miracles to free life and exercise of power; but this is precisely what a decided faith in the omnipresent and continually active divine government of the world cannot possibly admit. Besides, it would manifestly contradict the divine unchangeableness if He should work now according to order and again not according to order, now in founding and again in annulling the order of the world. And in particular, as we have recognised the order of nature as the *revelation* of the divine omnipotence, we cannot establish such an opposition between the one and the other as that God would be fettered or limited by the order of nature, and could now and again feel a need to break through or limit this fetter. As little as God is confined within limits by the moral order of the world, just as little is He so limited by the natural order. Both are in fact posited wholly and equally by His will, and are revelations of His eternal Logos—a violation of which would therefore be a self-contradiction of God, which is excluded by His eternal perfection. And as miracle contradicts the right conception of God, so does it also contradict the conception of Nature as the connection of causes and effects in conformity with law. Nor can appeal to our unacquaintedness with the individual laws of nature alter anything in this position; for a process which did not correspond to our known laws of nature, but which was to be explained from other laws of nature still unknown to us at the time, would on that account not be a real miracle, a supernatural occurrence and object of faith, but would be a problem of natural science, and therefore not of any direct religious significance. Nor can any valid argument be adduced from reference to the "elasticity of the laws of nature." The laws themselves are not elastic, but are inviolable necessities of working under given conditions. Wherever an expected effect does not or does not completely appear, we there assume as self-evident that collateral causes concurred with the principal causes, and that these checked or modified its operation; but even this check still takes place always according to determinate and calculable laws. When, for example, the astronomer Leverrier perceived deviations in the path of the planet Uranus which could not be explained from the positions of the planets hitherto known, he did not satisfy himself somehow with the assumption of elastic laws of nature, but he thought that the cause of the deviations lay in the influence of a planet not yet discovered at the time, the approximate place of which he accordingly determined; and this then led to the discovery of the planet Neptune. Were the laws of nature "elastic"—*i.e.*, did their working vary in an accidental and groundless way—then there would neither be possible an exact knowledge of nature nor a sure mode of action on the ground of the known laws of nature. With such a view we should be transported out of the real world, in which the order of events happens in accordance with law, into the fantastic world of fables and magic, where we should lose all our bearings both theoretical and practical.

If we must accordingly deny the reality of miracles in the strict super-naturalistic sense of the word, we cannot escape from the question how we are to explain the rise and significance of the *belief in miracle* in religion? Here, of course, it would not be in place to give an exhaustive answer to this question, which would lead us deep into the labyrinth of historical investigation. I should like to give only a few suggestive hints which seem fitted for the elucidation of the religious view of the world. Miraculous legends arise in a twofold way—partly out of the idealising of the real, and partly out of the realising of the ideal. Every occurrence, through whatever natural causes it is to be explained, may obtain for the religious judgment the significance of a "sign" or proof of the world-governing power, wisdom, justice, or goodness of God. This ideal significance, which the real cause does not at all exclude, rests upon the subjective interpretation of the occurrence, which interpretation is not arbitrary but describes the impression which the occurrence made upon the religious sense of the perceiver. But again, it is quite conceivable on psychological grounds that occurrences which have made a deep and lasting impression not merely on individuals but on whole circles of religiously excited men, become involuntarily *idealised*, even on the occasion of their being perceived by the first eyewitnesses, and still more in their recollection of them. That is to say, the features of the reality which are not essential, or which disturb the ideal impression, are suppressed, and the significant elevating features are heightened above the measure of the reality; or the intermediate members of an operation which withdraw themselves from the notice of the observer are suppressed, and a supernatural power is put into the place of the natural causal connection. Thus arise the relative miraculous histories, in which a real historical background is to be presupposed, but which was overlaid with mythical accessories by the idealising fantasy. It is in this way that the numberless half-historical and half-poetical "legends" in the history of religion may have arisen. But the religious spirit idealises not merely real occurrences of the external world; it also produces of its own spontaneity ideas and ideals to which nothing real in the outer world corresponds, but in which *only* inner living experiences of the pious soul, its struggles and triumphs, its beliefs and hopes, are brought to expression. These ideas are now involuntarily invested by the fantasy in symbolical images which are taken from the external world, but which, because they serve to give expression to a supersensible ideal, must themselves consist of supernatural processes. Thus are formed the purely ideal miracle-legends which have no external reality as their foundation, but in which only inner pious experiences, aspirations, and hopes of the soul find a symbolical figurative expression. Yet it must be carefully borne in mind that the religious fantasy, in producing such poetic symbolical legends, is not in the habit of distinguishing, nor can distinguish, between the ideal truth and its sensible investment. It becomes conscious of the ideal truth, not in a purely spiritual form and in abstract conceptions, but only in the sensible form of poetic intuition; and therefore it believes in the reality of the miraculous history produced by itself, with the same immediate certainty with which it is convinced of the truth of the religious idea contained in it. The history of all the higher religions, and in particular of Christianity, is rich in examples of such miraculous histories, in which the historical understanding can perceive nothing but a poetic realising of religious ideas. But in thus explaining the rise of these narratives out of psychological conditions and motives of the religious spirit of individuals and communities, we are far from that iconoclastic rationalism which combated miracles from an intellectual fanaticism, and made them contemptible, because it was not able to transport itself into the religious consciousness of past times. It is just the doctrine of development which is able to heal again the wounds which it inflicts upon simple faith; for it teaches us that even the highest spiritual truths can develop themselves only gradually in the human consciousness, and that it is a condition belonging to the laws of this development, that the spiritual invests itself at first in a sensible vesture, and only gradually frees itself from this disguise. Whoever has once apprehended this law is as far removed from wishing to destroy the husk prematurely before the fruit has ripened, as from desiring to defend the shell as a thing for ever necessary and not to be meddled with. To the matured faith the world itself is the one great miracle of the successive realising of the divine ideal; and therefore such faith honours in all miracle-legends the beautiful symbols of the one great miracle of the divine government of the world and of the education of humanity, that heavenly treasure which mankind could not hide otherwise than in earthen vessels. Thus for us too the words of Goethe hold true, that

"Miracle is faith's own dearest child."

LECTURE X.

THE RELIGIOUS VIEW OF THE WORLD.

II. OPTIMISM AND PESSIMISM.

WHAT is the origin of evil? whence has it come? This question has ever moved mankind, and it has been a leading motive in the formation of religious and philosophical theories. We may divide the answers to this question into three classes: (1) Evil has been referred back to an extra-divine principle—namely, either to one or many evil spirits, or to fate, or to matter—at all events to a principle limiting the divine power; (2) it has been referred to a want or defect in the Deity Himself, either to His imperfect wisdom or imperfect goodness; (3) it has been referred to human culpability, either to a universal imperfection of human nature or to particular transgressions of the first men.

It is easy to understand how in the *nature-religions* the beneficial and prejudicial operations of nature were ascribed to heterogeneous causes, and that the evil malevolent Gods and spirits were opposed to those that were good and beneficent. This *dualism* is found in some form in all nature-religions; the relationship of the evil world of spirits to the good, and the significance of the former for man, shaped itself very differently in the different religions, according to the more optimistic or more pessimistic disposition or mood of the peoples in question. In the case of savage tribes under unfavourable conditions of life, such as the African negroes, or in the case of half-civilised races which were maltreated by secular or priestly tyranny, like the Mexicans or the Indian Çiva-worshippers, or even in the case of the medieval Christians, the pessimistic mood predominates so much that their religion is more an agony of terror before the bad God than worship of the good God. The Egyptians and Western Semites thought less pessimistically, but always still badly enough of the power of the bad principle. In the cult of Osiris, of Adonis, Sandon, and Melkarth, the two hostile principles stand side by side on such a footing of equality that in the circle of the year alternately the one and the other conquers without a final victory being ever reached, and this is the purely naturalistic view of the world as void of history and purposeless.

Among the Iranians and Persians the hard struggle for existence which was forced upon them, by their geographical and historical situation, is likewise reflected in their dualistic heightening of the universal

Indo-Germanic opposition of spirits contrasted as light and dark, beneficial and prejudicial. The concentrating of the latter into one personal head in Angromainyu (Ahriman), who is almost on a footing of equality with Ahuramazda, was perhaps a consequence of the moralising of the old Iranian nature-religion by Zarathustra. Yet this dualism is not an absolute one, as the victory of Ahura is hoped for at the end of the world. Till then his worshippers have to take an active part in the struggle against the hostile kingdom of spirits, by the exercise of all religious and civil virtues. Civil morality holds good as an essential means for the fulfilment of the religious purpose, the victory of Ahura over Ahriman; but both this end and means still move essentially on the ground of the natural interests of the people; Ahura's honour is identical with the lordship of the Persian state. Corresponding to the rigid organisation and the martial spirit of the Persian military monarchy is the concentration of the hostile spirit-hosts in the personal heads—Ahura and Ahriman. Reflection is not yet directed to the fate of individuals in distinction from the whole of the people, or to the discrepancy between virtue and happiness; and thus the system still lacks the motives for the individual deepening of the religious view of the world.

The Greeks of the Homeric time are the classical example of naïve youthful optimism. So much the more instructive is the sudden dialectical change and transition which is to be observed in their case (as in that of the ethnologically related Indians), from the optimistic into the pessimistic mood of life and view of the world. To no nation had the terrestrial life taken shape with such cheerful and sunny radiance as to the Greek in the youthful days of its historical existence. The Greek mythology had transfigured the world into an idyl, in which Gods and men conversed with each other like beings of kindred nature. The Gods of this poetic idyl were the ideal forms of man, not because of the moral and spiritual perfectness of their being, but in virtue of the perfect beauty and inexhaustible fulness of their sensuous enjoyment of life. The stage on which Gods and men thus met was formed by those regions of the terrestrial world that lay under the sun's fairest glow. Yet no nation has in the end so completely transformed its view of the worth of life as the Greek nation did. The Greece that ends in the religious speculation of Neo-Pythagoreanism and Neo-Platonism regarded the same world which had once appeared to it so full of joy and light, as a place of darkness and error, and the earthly existence as a time of probation which cannot be quickly enough passed through. The beginning of this turn of view lay far back; it may almost be found already in Hesiod's description of the ages ever becoming worse. The more, then, the poets and thinkers of the classic time of Greece rose to the thought of the moral order of the world, so much the more did their observation of the misrelation between fate and guilt become to them a painful riddle, which was not solved, but only made more acute, by the popular belief in fate or in the envy of the Gods. In the case of Sophocles especially every tragedy was a new exhibition of this mystery of the world, a new question raised as to the unintelligible rule of the Gods. Sophocles expressed his own doubt of the justice of the world in the words of Antigone: "How can I, in my wretchedness, still look to the Gods? whom can I invoke as a helper, as an ally, seeing that I have drawn upon myself the curse of godlessness by my fear of the Gods?" These doubts sought at first their solution in the idea of retribution in the world beyond, by which Hades, hitherto thought of as indifferent, was differentiated into places of reward and punishment. But in the same measure in which the life in the future world gained in interest and worth, the life in the present world lost value. This is already distinctly betrayed in the words of Antigone when she says that she has to give more heed to the departed, with whom she will always be in future, than to those of this world. These moods and views, which were pre-eminently cherished in the cult of the mysteries, were fully carried out after Socrates by the idealistic philosophy. Plato taught that the terrestrial world is only a shadowy and deformed copy of the world of ideas, and that our body is a prison, out of which the soul, which springs from above, has to raise itself to the world of ideas. The earthly life had, for this thinker, only the significance of a preparation for the better life in the world beyond. The Stoics likewise, although starting from other theoretical presuppositions, yet came practically to a quite similar estimation of the natural goods of life. The wise man, as they taught, can only find the highest good of full rest of soul in liberation from all natural passions, in the mortification of the heart, and indifference to all cares and joys. The rational self-consciousness returns here into itself from all that is external as from something alien and hostile, in order to find, in its own pure inwardness and freedom, harmony with itself and with the absolute world-reason, and therewith the highest good. But in this proud self-glorification and depreciation of the external world, the solitary Ego empties itself of all definite content, even of all moral values and ends; there remains only the abstract self, which is null and worthless in its emptiness. Hence this world-despising pessimism of the Stoics is always on the point of despising and throwing away even the individual's own life, as equally worthless with the rest of the world. As the world was formerly negated for the sake of the self, so even the self is at last negated along with the rest of the world. In such absolute pessimism and illusionism did the original absolute optimism of the Greeks end.

Quite analogous, but still more logical and extreme, in the case of the Indians, was the passage from the original optimism of the deification of nature into the final absolutely pessimistic negation of the world. Politics, religion, and philosophy here contributed in equal parts to bring the Indian people, which had once been full of the joy of life and activity, to contempt of the world and to disgust of life. Their civil life was without lasting and great ends—a constant change of petty tyrants, who split up society by the barriers of the castes, without national common feeling. Nor did the world beyond furnish here, as in the Greek mysteries, a scant comfort for the sad life of the present, as the doctrine of the transmigration of souls threatened to prolong the circulation of wretched existence without end. The Brahmanic philosophy had always been strong only in the abstracting and resolving of all that is particular into an empty universality, whose highest is Brahma. Instead of conceiving and ordering the chaos of existence under a supreme principle, it sublimated it into an All-One, of which nothing can be further said than that it is the alone existing being, while the world of the particular is empty seeming and deception. From this speculative negation of the world *Gautama Buddha* then drew its practical and popular consequence. All life, according to Buddha, is suffering; for it is desire of the soul for goods that are naught, and which by their transitoriness prepare a constant illusion. Hence man has to make himself free from all desiring, to become wishless and hopeless, in order to find peace, rest, Nirvâna. But with this evacuation of all the content of life, man at last also loses himself. This consequence, which the Stoics occasionally drew by practical suicide, Buddha drew as a demand in principle, not indeed for bodily but for spiritual self-mortification. Whoever would become free from the evil of the illusion of the external world, must at last also become free from the fundamental evil, from the illusion of one's own existence. All willing and thinking must die out and expire from want of spiritual nourishment, and then the peace of the Nirvâna first takes up its abode, a peace which no breath of evil any more affects. This is the most radical pessimism thinkable; but it contains at the same time its own *reductio ad absurdum*. For it is a self-contradiction that the self-conscious Ego should think itself as *not* being, and should will as *not* willing. Thus we have seen how, among the Greeks and Indians, the original optimism of a crude idolatry of the world turned round at last in a quite similar way into an extreme pessimism, which again shows itself to be untenable, because it cannot be carried out without self-contradiction. With this, history has itself already pronounced the judgment that neither upon the one nor upon the other side alone can the truth be found.

But history has also shown the positive overcoming of both errors in the development of the religion of

Israel. This people also started from a simple optimism. "God saw all that He had made, and behold it was very good;" and He gave over the earth and what is in it to men, that they should govern it. In particular, God chose the people of Israel to be His own people, and He concluded a covenant with it with mutual obligation. Israel was to be God's holy people, and in consideration of this the possession of the land of Canaan and all earthly prosperity was promised to it. This idea of the covenant of God ruled the historical pragmatism of the prophets of Israel. From this point of view they explained the evils from which their people had often to suffer as just punishments of God for the unfaithfulness of Israel, but yet at the same time as means for the purification of the people, in order to lead it towards its ideal of a holy people of God. The basis of their ethical monotheism forbade them to think of a blind fate, or of the envy of the Deity. But this explanation of evils from the retributive justice of God sufficed only so long as the religious reflection was limited to the people as a whole. On the other hand, as soon as the postulate of just retribution was applied to individuals, it was impossible to avoid seeing that it was the most just—those who participated least in the guilt of the people, nay, even those who had resisted it most staunchly—who had often nevertheless to suffer most, while the unjust enjoyed good fortune. With this position there was also raised for the Jewish piety the question of the theodicy, which on the basis of ethical monotheism has its peculiar difficulty — namely, How is the experienced misrelation of morality and fate to be made to tally with the government of an almighty and a just God? The author of the Book of Job has struggled with this problem, but he was unable to solve it. The explanation of the friends of Job, that his misfortunes pointed to hidden guilt, is declared to be false, seeing that God Himself recognises the innocence of Job. But the question as to the ground of his misfortunes is simply smitten down in the poetical conclusion as unjustified and insoluble for the human understanding: "I will lay mine hand upon my mouth and be silent, for these things are too high for me, and cannot be understood." In the narrative conclusion, on the other hand, Job is at last richly indemnified by reparation of all his losses. And thus the narrator falls back again into the old theory of retribution, whose insufficiency, because of its contrariety to experience, had just been the occasion of the whole raising of the problem. While in the Book of Job doubt still struggles with faith, in the Book of Ecclesiastes despair of the just government of the world is the ruling mood: "All things come alike to all: there is one event to the righteous, and to the wicked; to the good and to the clean, and to the unclean. So I returned, and considered all the oppressions that are done under the sun; and behold the tears of such as were oppressed, and they had no comforter; and on the side of their oppressors there was power. I have seen all the works that are done under the sun; and, behold, all is vanity and vexation of spirit." Amid this lamentation of the present, the questioning gaze does indeed direct itself to the world beyond; but here too it ends with anxious doubt: "Who knoweth whether the spirit of man goeth upward?"

Yet with such hopeless resignation the Jewish piety could not stop; for its essence was a hopeful idealism, a trusting in the faithfulness and righteousness of God, who must yet at last lead His good cause and that of His faithful ones to victory, although the way to this goal leads through suffering. During the suffering time of the Exile, when the most pious had to endure the greatest suffering, yet also contributed most by their patient perseverance to the salvation and establishment of the people, there was formed the new ideal of the "pious endurer" (Anav), who, under external debasement, poverty, and oppression, nevertheless ceases not to wait for the consolation of Israel, and who does not allow himself to be shaken in his pious trust in God, although he no longer himself experiences external prosperity. The inner certainty of fellowship with his God is his consolation and compensation even in continuing external misfortune: "Whom have I in heaven but Thee? and there is none upon earth that I desire besides Thee. My flesh and my heart faileth:

but God is the strength of my heart, and my portion for ever" (Ps. lxxiii. 25, 26). Thus did the Jewish piety purify itself in the case of individuals in the fire of affliction from the dross of its earthly mercenariness, and it gained in its internal deepening a self-certainty and satisfaction which was independent of the chance of external fatalities, and was no longer exposed to doubt. It is true that it was indeed always only but a few select spirits who were able to raise themselves to such religious idealism; and even for them the hope still stood fast that the cause of God could not be for ever the vanquished one, but that it must some day conquer even in the external world, and right come to power and dominion. But the more the reality appeared to stand in contradiction with this postulate, so much the more did the hope of a miraculous future, when it was contrasted with the present course of the world, direct itself towards a super-terrestrial world beyond, to a "kingdom of the Saints" coming down from heaven to earth, in the glory of which those who had died in the intervening time should also obtain their share by their resurrection from the dead. Since the time of the Maccabees the Jewish faith rose above the distress of the present to the hope of a transcendent adjustment, which transported into the far distance its original earthly realism and optimism. At the same time, however, this displacement of the religious ideal into a future that was to be miraculously established, and which did not naturally cohere with the present, had the consequence that now the present appeared always only the gloomier in contrast to this high-flying ideal representation of the future. The Apocalyptic transcendence of the future Messianic age had corresponding to it, as its obverse side, the dominion of the realm of demons in the earthly present.

As little as the hope of a resurrection, had the fear of demons been an original element of the Hebrew religion. Even if it were the case that the belief in spirits was not foreign to the ancient Hebrews, it had undoubtedly nothing to do with the Jahve-religion. There was first formed in the post-Exilian time, probably under the influence of the Persian dualism, the idea of a kingdom of impure hostile spirits with *Satan* or Beelzebub at their head. In Job he still stands among the sons of God as the accuser of the pious, but yet strictly subordinated to God. According to 1 Chronicles xxi. 1, Satan induced David to undertake the fatal numbering of the people; the author of which, according to the earlier notion (2 Samuel xxiv. 1), had, however, been God Himself. We see from this how the idea of the Devil was a welcome expedient for the need of an advanced religious reflection, to put God out of relation to the evil and badness of the world. In the Apocryphal and Apocalyptic writings of the last pre-Christian time, the demonology occupies always larger room. The whole of heathenism was regarded by the Jews as the sphere of the dominion of the demons; and when the heathen empire of the Romans reduced the Jewish people also under its sceptre, Satan appeared forthwith as "the prince of this world," to whom God has assigned the present world-age, but in order to take again into His hands the government of the world on the occasion of the miraculous establishment of the Messianic kingdom in the new age. So comfortless and godless did the actual world appear to the Jews of the last century before the destruction of Jerusalem, that they could see in it only the kingdom of Satan, the direct opposite of the kingdom of God, which on that very account was to enter into existence only through miraculous catastrophes. The view that the real world is very good, from which Israel had started in the time of the prophets, had given place here too, not less than with the Greeks and Indians, to a pessimistic despair of the real world. Yet what distinguished this Jewish pessimism from the Greek and Indian was the firm hope that the misery would not last for ever, but that a new better world would soon dawn, in which God would wipe away all tears from the eyes of the pious.

Christianity also started from this same pessimistic view of the world, but it made it the foil of its doctrine of redemption and salvation. It did not weaken the feeling for the great power of the physical and moral evils in the world, but it put in prospect the overcoming of them through the kingdom of God which is dawning, and it set its forces to work. Jesus knew by the healing power of His word over those who were diseased in body and soul, whom He also regarded as tormented by demons, that the kingdom of God had now come (Luke xi. 20); that a stronger One had come to rule over Satan and his kingdom, who would bind him, and spoil his house. He saw Satan fall like lightning from heaven (Luke x. 18)—that is to say, He saw his power over the world broken by the force of the faith which in full surrender to God gives freedom from the power of men and demons: "All things are possible to him that believeth." Jesus was far from the shallow optimism which ignores the power of the bad and expects an easy victory of the good without a struggle. He knew that suffering was His own lot and that of His followers in the world; but He knew also that sufferings borne in pious obedience to God become means for the victory of the good, for the salvation of the individual and of the whole: "For whosoever will save his life shall lose it; but whosoever shall lose his life for my sake and the Gospel's, the same shall save it. For even the Son of man came not to be ministered unto, but to minister, and to give His life a ransom for many" (Mark viii. 35, x. 45). In this certainty of faith that even the worst evils of the world are at last only means for the good purposes of God, lay the victory which has overcome the world—which in the first place overcame it internally, in that it made the pious man free from the terror of the world, and made him strong for the struggle against all godless things. And the same mood passes through the whole of the New Testament, and especially through the Epistles of the apostle Paul. "We know that all things work together for good to them that love God. If God be for us, who can be against us? I am persuaded that neither death, nor life, nor any other creature, shall be able to separate us from the love of God. As sorrowful, yet always rejoicing; as poor, yet making many rich; as having nothing, and yet possessing all things" (Romans viii. 28, 38 f.; 2 Cor. vi. 10 f.) This is the fundamental mood of the Christian in presence of the evils of the world—as far removed from shallow optimism, which does not, or will not, see the power of evil and badness, and to which much frivolity or hardness of heart belongs, as from the despondent pessimism which despairs of the victory of the good in the world, and consequently also paralyses the power for earnest conflict and deadens the heart in dull indifference.

The Christian view of the world proves itself to be the true view also by the fact that it combines the highest idealism, belief in the world-governing power of the good, with the common-sense realism which sees the world as it actually is. The Christian is not an abstract idealist who in visionary optimism holds the world simply to be excellent, all that is actual to be rational, and even evil and badness to be mere seeming, or a shadow fitted for beautifying the whole picture. His heart is not so hard and unfeeling that he does not feel his own and others' suffering as real woe; his conscience is not so obtuse that he could approve evil and see peace where there is no peace. On the contrary, because he never judges men and things according to the external appearance, but according to the internal reality, he perceives wrong and error in much that appears to others as right and good; his attitude towards reality is always in a certain respect critical and polemical, because he measures it by his ideal, and he cannot overlook the distance of the actuality from what ought to be. But with all this, to him it is not less firmly established that the world, in spite of all its imperfectness, is the work of God, the object of His redeeming love, the place of His coming kingdom. On the one hand, he knows that we are not to love the world nor what is in it, for the world with its fashion passes away; and, on the other hand, he believes that God has loved the world and reconciled it with Himself,—that all is from God, and through Him, and to Him! In this wonderful *antinomy* lies the enigma, lies the strength of Christianity. The practical solution of this enigma was indeed always present in the immediate experience of the pious soul, in the faith which felt God's power present in all human weakness, in the love which put forth its hand to further the divine kingdom upon earth, and in the hope which soared over the afflictions of time to the glory which is yet to be revealed in us. Nevertheless, there lay in that antinomy a problem for the religious reflection, the solution of which could not be quite satisfactorily attained at the very outset.

In the *primitive Christianity* the pessimistic polemical side of the Christian estimation of the world strongly predominated, and it expressed itself in an ascetic attitude, not merely towards the life of sense, but also towards the higher life of the world. The primitive Christianity loosened man from the earthly bonds and interests of society, from family and country, from law and State, from art and science, by showing him his true home in heaven. This partly arose from the historical relationships of the society of the time, in which even the higher human endeavours had undergone such deep moral corruption that no other than a polemical attitude towards them was possible, unless the Christian ideal was to be lowered by false compromises. But the ground of the world-denying pessimism and asceticism of the primitive Christianity lay partly also in the abstract supernaturalism which it had taken possession of as an inheritance from the Jewish Apocalyptic. For, according to the Apocalyptic representation of the kingdom of God, that kingdom was not to grow out of the historical life of man, but was to break its continuity, and to enter into existence by a direct divine intervention from heaven. From this it followed naturally that the present world, up to the coming of Christ and His heavenly kingdom, still appeared as the mere opposite of that kingdom, as a place of powers hostile to God. Augustine called the Roman empire a *civitas diaboli;* and the whole Greek culture was, in the eyes of Tertullian, a *pompa diaboli*. Thus there was continued in Christianity the dualist-pessimistic view of the world which had been the final result of the ancient development of civilisation, and this view was carried forward in it for centuries. Not that the specifically Christian truth of the reconciliation of God and of the world had on that account been forgotten; but it was, as it were, hermetically sealed in the mystery of its dogma and worship. To the real world outside of the Church this truth did not hold good; for that world remained, in the eyes of the Christians, after as before the coming of Christ, God-forsaken and governed by demons. The terror of the devil and diabolical magic grew in the middle ages to an even more morbid height than it had ever reached in the pre-Christian world, having been intensified by the struggle of the Church with the heathenism outside as well as within its boundaries, and by the amalgamation of heresy with witchcraft, in connection with which the Church used the popular superstition as a weapon for the suppression of her opponents.

In the sixteenth century began the reaction from this dualistic pessimistic view of the world, and it started at the same time from two sides. In the *Renaissance* the world established its claim to the independent worth of the goods of civilisation outside of the Church, of scientific truth and artistic beauty; in the *Reformation* Christianity loosened itself from its ecclesiastical bonds and its ascetic enmity to the world. The gulf between the kingdom of God and the world was bridged over by that kingdom being no longer limited to the Church, but extended to the moral community generally, and by the world being liberated from the ban of unholiness, and being recognised as the nursery-ground of the moral goods of Christianity. Certainly there was still much wanting to the complete and logical carrying through of this view of the desecularising and reconciliation of the world with Christianity. There acted as a hindrance to it the continuing authority of the old ecclesiastical dogma with its abstract supernaturalism, whose natural consequence was the dualism of the spiritual and the secular. Besides this, the medieval terror of the devil lasted in Protestantism for three centuries, and bore its evil fruits in the horrors of the prosecutions of witches. It was the second Renaissance at the end of the eighteenth century that first carried out theoretically and practically the reconciliation of spirit and nature which had begun in the sixteenth century; and in connection with it, it is easy to understand that the recoil from the ecclesiastical supernaturalism led at first to a half-heathen naturalism and optimistic deification of the world. Rousseau's preaching of the excellence of human nature and of the return to the simplicity of the state of nature as the means of salvation from all evils, found everywhere enthusiastic followers. But when the French Revolution had translated this theory into practice, the disillusion was the more bitter the more naïve the enthusiasm for nature had been. Then there followed after the optimism of the eighteenth century the poetical world-pain of Byron, which Schopenhauer has raised to the philosophical creed of pessimism.

Certainly one is justified in seeing in the pessimistic philosophy of Schopenhauer and his followers a product and reflection of the mood of the age, which, disillusionised from the transcendental Utopias of abstract idealism and sobered down, has become realistic and resigned. Nevertheless, it ought not to be overlooked that this philosophy is in certain respects a consequence of the Kantian dualism, which held the good to be unattainable and the true to be incognisable. There is, according to Kant, such an absolute discordance between reason and the sensibility, that the ideas of the pure reason only entangle the understanding, which is bound to the senses, in insoluble dialectical contradictions, and that the moral demands of reason find themselves in eternal conflict with the actual desire of the sensible nature of man; so that duty and inclination can never go together, and the highest good set up as a task by reason must always be only an ideal goal, and never realised. If this be so, it was a very natural inference that was drawn by Schopenhauer—namely, that the substance of the world is the irrational will, and that its existence is therefore in irreconcilable discord with the rational idea and is consequently an evil, before whose insuperable power nothing remains to us but the resigned "negation of the will to live," the Buddhistic Nirvâna. But we have already seen how this theory led in the Indian philosophy itself to absurdity: the same thing may be here noticed again under a new point of view. If all our willing is an effluence of the irrational world-will, then all our purposive conceptions or ideals are in like manner irrational, have therefore no claim to truth and validity, nor can they be applied as a rule for the estimation of reality. With this, however, falls away all possibility of a rational estimation of reality; and consequently Schopenhauer's negative judgment regarding the worth of the world becomes also groundless and arbitrary. Or conversely: if we are to be in a position to pronounce rational judgments (whatever be their issue) concerning the worth of the world, then we must measure it by an ideal conception of whose rational truth we are convinced; but if we are able to form rational ideal conceptions, then our willing cannot be wholly reasonless; but if there is reason in our willing, which is a weak and limited effluence of the world-will, there must also surely be reason in the *world*-will; but then the world, as a product of the rational world-will, cannot be an irrational evil, but must be a means for the realising of the ideal, which could not be *our* purposive thought, unless it were also the primal purposive thought of the world-will itself, and therefore the final cause of the real. In short, pessimism as a philosophy breaks to pieces on the inner contradiction that it denies the rationality of the world and yet assumes the rationality of its judging about the world, which is yet also a constituent element of the whole; or that it denies the tendency of the world to the good, and yet in its own forming of ideals it proves actually the existence and activity of that very tendency. Hence pessimism as a form of thought always appears when thinking performs its inexorable criticism on the objective world, but the subject is so completely merged in this critical process that it forgets itself therein, and does not perceive that it already has *in itself* what it seeks and misses without; nay more, that its seeking it is itself a sign of the hidden existence of what is sought for, and consequently the guarantee also of its coming to be found.

The rising of this consciousness was the salvation which Christianity brought to the pessimistically world-weary humanity, with its message that the kingdom of

God is not merely a future far-off ideal, but that it is already a present reality within, in the hearts of the children of God. The opposition of reality and Ideal, of the world and the kingdom of God, is indeed not denied, yet it is no longer the whole truth, but only *one* side of it,—the starting-point, which is to be, and can be, raised to unity. But the theoretical mediation of the two sides contained in the Christian principle was not yet possible under the presuppositions of the Apocalyptic supernaturalism. For us it becomes possible through the conception of development, which enables us to know in the real the becoming of the ideal, and in the ideal the final cause of the real. These two things stand equally established to us,— that the kingdom of God, or the ideal of the universal highest good, transcends all bounded reality, and yet that the reality always already participates in it in some measure, in so far as it contains the germs out of which the Ideal is to develop itself. From this point of view even the evil of the world loses its painful sting, and transforms itself into a co-operating means for the bringing forth of the good.

That the good can only develop itself in conflict with its opposite, and consequently at the price of pain, can be most clearly recognised when we reflect upon the personal life. If man is to attain to a morally good will corresponding to the rational order of the universe, the natural impulses must be restrained and overcome in their immediate exercise, and made subject to the higher end. Without the struggle with one's own nature, without the pain of self-conquest, no virtue is possible. Ὁ μὴ δαρεὶς ἄνθρωπος οὐ παιδεύεται. Nor is this to be accomplished merely by a single heroic act of renunciation of the self-will, but the moral ideal demands daily new labour upon ourselves and the sacrifice of self-subdual. With every step in the progress of moral insight grow also the demands and tasks of the moral life; no standing still, no idle letting alone, is permitted. It is only the faithful one who perseveres unweariedly in toil and conflict, who wins the crown of moral perfection. But what holds true of the individual life, holds in a still greater degree of the whole life of the peoples and of mankind. For the more complicated a moral organism is, so much the more difficult is it to establish and to preserve the harmonious order of its manifold directions of will. Here it is not merely individual natural impulses that stand over against each other, but the morally justified interests of life in the different groups of society struggle with each other for the supremacy; the wellbeing of the people as a whole must be purchased by sacrifice of the individuals. The severest conflicts and sufferings for the people, however, grow out of the progress of the moral and religious modes of thinking and feeling. When old practices and dogmas are felt to be untrue and unright, and new ideals of a civil or ecclesiastical kind are endeavouring to obtain validity, then arises the struggle between the existing order, which has been consecrated by the authority of the Fathers, and the bearers of the new ideas. Here it is not wrong that stands against right, but it is the right of the past which stands against the right of the future. It is the idea which has embodied itself in the actuality of the public life, and which has authenticated its vitality— which indeed it has already more or less exhausted— it is this idea which stands in opposition to the other idea which would now first realise itself, and which has yet to prove its capacity of life. These are the hardest, the truly tragic, oppositions and struggles of the world's history, out of which the bitterest pains of humanity have grown at all times. But how could humanity have been spared these sufferings if it is to develop all its innate capacities and approach the ideal of an all-embracing harmony, the ideal of a divine-human organism or kingdom? "Ought not Christ to have suffered these things, and to enter into His glory?" This fate of the greatest of the sons of men is typical of the fate of the whole of mankind. Viewed in its light, the whole history of the world appears as a single magnificent Theodicy, and all the sufferings of peoples and individuals are transfigured into means of salvation. All the battlefields of the world's history, and all the martyr-pyres of the Church's past, become sacrificial altars upon which man has offered his sacrifices in order to purchase his redemption from the slavery of vanity, and his elevation to the glory of the liberty of the children of God.

If we can thus combine the worst evils which accrue to humanity from its own historical development, with the teleology of the divine order of the world and salvation, then the comparatively smaller evils which arise to it from the order of nature will no longer present any insuperable difficulty. In so far as man is a natural being, he must also share the lot of all flesh; he must suffer death and other natural evils. And to these evils he is exposed even more than the beasts, because he is more finely—and therefore more sensitively—organised, and because he is more helpless and defenceless in his isolation than they are. But this very physical defencelessness of his compelled him from the beginning to enter into social union, and led him thereby into the path of civilisation. His more sensitive organism, however, is connected with his intelligence, in which he possesses the victorious weapon for the domination of nature. The sufferings inflicted by external nature, which the beast only passively endures, become for man means of stimulation which incite his senses to lasting attention and his understanding to reflection, to meditative observation and anticipative calculation. But by means of observation and reflection man gradually learns in the course of time by listening to nature to make out her laws, and to employ her forces for his own ends. The whole history of civilisation is an advancing victory of the human spirit over crude nature, a victory which he would never have reached without the constant spur of physical evils. Nature thus proves herself, not less in her beneficial than in her prejudicial operations, the means which excellently serves the end of the spirit,—the granite foundation upon whose fast-ordered structure man is able to erect the edifice of his civilisation, the temple of the eternal spirit. How then can we complain about this order of nature which bears the whole human existence with all its spiritual goods, because out of its ordered course in detail there also proceeds many a check and destruction to the happiness of human life? Ought not the experience of the inevitableness of natural evils, which indeed, in spite of all the progress of civilisation, are yet not wholly spared to any mortal, rather serve to give us the wholesome warning that man's highest goal and good is not to be sought in the world of sense, but in the world of the spirit, whose eternal good things are not affected by the happenings and changes of the course of nature?

If we take all these considerations together, we shall now be able to say that the true religious optimism, as Christianity understands it, does not consist in this, that the actual is to be held without further consideration as good, nor that the evil in it is to be ignored; but it consists in this, that the actual world is to be viewed as a teleological process of development, through which the good, the divine world-purpose, always realises itself more and more — a process of development from which, however, evils are so little excluded that they rather serve as necessary and wholesome means for the good, which can only realise itself through their subdual. In this view of the world, in which resignation and trust are combined, consists also the kernel of the religious *belief in Providence*. In some sense or other it is found in all religions, inasmuch as belief in some sort of divine government in human things is inseparably connected with the belief in God generally. But upon heathen soil the belief in Providence always remains wavering and uncertain, partly because of the want of the unity of the divine will, and partly, in particular, because of the want of a single and moral world-purpose. Plato and the later Stoics—Seneca, Epictetus, Marcus Aurelius—approached most nearly to the Biblical belief in Providence, yet even they did not attain to the clear thought of a positive moral final end of the world; and hence in their belief in Providence the mood of resignation always again breaks through above that of trust. It was in the ethical Monotheism of the Hebrew prophets that the belief in Providence first rose to the conviction of a divine government of the world which aimed at the realising of moral final ends. Nevertheless these ends were at first rather national than purely and universally human. In the Psalms the prophetic belief in Providence individualised itself into the consciousness of a personal union with God, and consequently also into a divine guidance of the individual life. Christianity has spiritually deepened the belief in Providence exhibited in the Psalms, and it has partly expanded it universally; for it has found the life-purpose of the individual in his participation in the universal spiritual good of the kingdom of God, the final end of the divine government of the world. The individual belief in Providence contained in the Psalms is combined in Christianity with the social belief in which it took form in the Prophets. Now, however, it is no longer nationally limited, but is expanded so as to embrace mankind as a whole, and so that the spiritual salvation of all is recognised as the purpose of the divine love, for the realisation of which the whole course of the world is ordered by the divine wisdom. And according to this its religious kernel, the belief in Providence is unassailable, and has no refutation to fear either from experience or from scientific knowledge of the world.

The belief in Providence, however, inevitably comes into conflict with the realistic view of the world whenever Providence is referred to egoistically limited ends, which depend upon natural conditions, and which consequently could be brought about only by the interferences of an abstract supernatural Omnipotence with the ordered course of nature. Where such interferences by Providence are expected, disillusions cannot fail to come, and these have as their consequence doubt of Providence generally. It is a quite natural dialectic, in which one may almost perceive a just Nemesis, that the presumptuous supernaturalism which would put the omnipotence of the government of the world at the disposal of the individual for his own narrow limited purposes, reverts under the disillusions of actual experience into the radical unbelief of a naturalism which recognises nothing higher behind the causal necessity of the course of nature, and ends in heathen comfortlessness. On the other hand, if Providence is apprehended in the truly Christian sense that the whole natural and historical order of the world is the means for the realisation of the universal highest end,—the ideal humanity,—then not only does this religious view of the world stand in no contradiction with the intellectual knowledge of the connection of things in conformity with law, but the two views complete each other, as teleology and causalism form all over only the two sides of the *one* truth. For the mechanism of the causal connection is nowhere an end in itself. It is not the ultimate meaning of the world, but only the ministering instrument ($\mu\eta\chi\alpha\nu\acute{\eta}$) for the system of spiritual and moral ends which stands over it. If, then, according to the Christian belief in Providence, the *whole* of the world in its course in time is ordered to serve the highest end of the divine government of the world, or the kingdom of the divinely-good, as the means of its realisation, then it is self-evident that all *individual* happening, which belongs to the connection of the whole and is naturally caused in it, can and must also serve as a ministering means for that same highest end. And seeing that in the universal purpose, as the common highest good of humanity, the true good of all individuals is also included, it is a logical conclusion that all events which affect the individual in his particular course of life are to be viewed and turned to account as furthering means also for the fulfilment of his highest personal purpose in life. As Paul says, "All things work together for good to them that love God" (Romans viii. 28). To him who estimates life generally from the highest

tion in human point of view of the divine purpose, all the experiences of life obtain the significance of a God-ordered means of education and salvation. This sentiment, which combines resignation with elevation, humbleness with confidence and power, is the practical verification of the religious view of the world. "Our faith is the victory which has overcome the world."

END OF THE FIRST VOLUME.

PRINTED BY WILLIAM BLACKWOOD AND SONS.

www.ingramcontent.com/pod-product-compliance
Lightning Source LLC
Chambersburg PA
CBHW030006240426
43672CB00007B/841